"*God's Plan for Your Marriage* is a remarkable expression of the priestly mission which, in imitation of the Public Ministry of Christ the High Priest, is, first and foremost, at the service of the sacrament of Holy Matrimony and its incomparable fruit, the family. Inspired and sustained by the Virgin Mother of God, Fr. Robert J. Altier illustrates God's plan for marriage from the beginning, from the first moment of the creation of man—male and female—in God's own image, after His likeness. He shows how God the Father, through the Redemptive Incarnation of God the Son, gives us the sevenfold gift of God the Holy Spirit to live faithfully and generously according to the plan that He unfailingly writes upon every human heart."

—Raymond Leo Cardinal Burke

"There is a dearth of Catholic voices that can be trusted these days due to the modernism that has infected both clergy and laity. Today, the single biggest attack from Satan is against marriage and the family. Fr. Altier is one of those few voices I trust that will speak with moral clarity those inconvenient truths that laymen need to hear. His book goes against the prevailing 'zeitgeist,' and he provides the principles of how to live a God-centered marriage. This is critical for the survival of marriage. The book *God's Plan for your Marriage* is Catholic theology not only grounded on firm Scriptural foundation but also written in a way that Joe Six-Pack in the pew can understand. This book writes convincingly about the beauty and dignity of marriage. It will renew and purify your understanding of the first sacrament God instituted in the Garden of Eden. This book demonstrates that marriage is the normal means that God has given most Catholics to become holy. This book reinforced in my mind what I learned from Venerable Fulton Sheen decades ago, that it takes "three to get married": a man, a woman, and God—with God being the center, the apex, and the bond between husband and wife."

—Jesse and Anita Romero,
Virgin Most Powerful Radio

"The Great Saint John Paul II once famously said that "A *Love that leads to marriage is a gift from God and a great act of faith toward other human beings.*" Marriage today is both misunderstood and under attack. Satan hates it! That's why Fr. Altier's book is essential reading for anyone contemplating marriage as well as those who have already entered the sacrament. This is a gift that will help you better understand God's intention for marriage and the fulfillment He desires for you.

—Drew and Cathy Mariani,
Relevant Radio

"In our culture, which champions self-centered and disposable 'love,' this book, *God's Plan for Your Marriage*, is a breath of fresh air. From beginning to end, it is filled with wisdom. As I read through it, I was awed by Fr. Altier's insights into Sacred Scripture, the Church's teaching, and Theology of the Body. As I read through the book, I was deeply challenged and convicted of my own self-centeredness throughout the years of my marriage. This book is desperately needed in our time. Everyone who is married, or planning to marry, needs to read this. It will save them much heartache. This book will also be a source of healing for those who have gone through the pains of divorce or broken relationships. Finally, this book should be required reading for marital therapists and for everyone who helps prepare couples for marriage."

—Bob Schuchts,
Founder of the John Paul II Healing Center

God's Plan for Your Marriage

Fr. Robert J. Altier

God's Plan for Your Marriage

An Exploration of Holy Matrimony
from Genesis to the
Wedding Feast of the Lamb

SOPHIA INSTITUTE PRESS
Manchester, New Hampshire

Sophia Institute Press
Box 5284, Manchester, NH 03108
1-800-888-9344
www.SophiaInstitute.com

Sophia Institute Press is a registered trademark of Sophia Institute.

paperback ISBN 978-1-64413-692-8

ebook ISBN 978-1-64413-693-5

Library of Congress Control Number: 2022936785

4th printing

To our Lady, St. Joseph,
and all the married saints

Contents

Foreword

Sr. Lucia, one of the visionaries at Fátima, in a letter to the late Cardinal Caffarra, stated, "Father, a time will come when the decisive battle between the Kingdom of Christ and Satan will be over marriage and the family. And those who work for the good of the family will experience persecution and tribulation. But do not be afraid, because our Lady has already crushed his head." There is no need to recount statistics to prove to anyone that the family has disintegrated in dramatic fashion since Sr. Lucia penned that letter only decades ago. No Catholic needs to be convinced of this because we all stand in the midst of the rubble. There is no denying the disaster we face and the pain we see and suffer every day.

Even so, there is hope and evidence of God's renewal of the family in our time. Traditional families, families that cling to Jesus and His teachings, are living and experiencing the life-changing fruits of orienting their lives around the altar of God—the presence of God—the forgiveness of God. Thus, in their midst we find divorce rates that are dramatically lower than those who live outside of magisterial teaching. Their families and parishes are thriving. They do not rely on modern, godless pop psychology, Christianity lite, or secularism. Instead, they are turning to traditional liturgy and traditional living. They seek to order their families to the design revealed by and blessed by God.

What is the path they are following to all of this positive change? Aside from traditional liturgy, the practice of NFP, and so forth, what is lighting the way for them? Well, the truth is, most are just doing the best they can to navigate this path. To our knowledge, there is no single book about families and married life that can help them make this change. St. John Paul II's works on the Theology of the Body are a great help to those seeking to deepen their understanding of sex and sexuality. We are also guided by the joyful, healthy aspects of traditional Catholic culture, which have their roots in ancient Israel. Yet, until now, there has been little aid specifically for marriage that draws from the deep wells of tradition and prayer Fr. Altier, and the book you are holding, is a turning point.

How can a priest, who has never been married, understand marriage or help me with my marriage in any way? This question has probably crossed the minds of many over the centuries and may cross the mind of those wondering if this book will help them. Our answer is not complex. Priests grow up in families. When their vocations are healthy, they constantly serve and support families. They hear the confessions of family members of all personalities and ages. Priests are, in fact, more objective observers of the deepest issues in family and married life than those of any other profession are.

Though these factors are true with Fr. Altier, the answer regarding the wisdom found here is only partly rooted in his experience as a priest who cares deeply about marriage and the family. It also emanates from his decades of experience as an exorcist dealing with the deepest, darkest corners of our humanity and the spiritual realm. He has learned what binds and hinders the soul and what truly sets it free. As a man who has faced down the demons that afflict marriage, he knows all the tactics of the enemy and the corresponding tools and perspectives we need to be set free. This, too, is a well from which he has drawn to provide the wisdom you will find in this book.

The most important source that any humble author would be uncomfortable revealing is that this book, in its primary inspiration, was birthed out of a deep place of prayer and union with God. We know Fr. Altier personally and have interacted with him for a number of years. The fruit of his ministry is unquestionable. And we believe that this book emerged from a source that breaks through only in the heart of one who is deeply united with God and the Blessed Mother. We would even go so far as to suggest that this book was inspired by the Holy Spirit. When time demands a prophetic voice, as it does now, God speaks. We believe He has spoken through Fr. Altier in this book and that anyone who entrusts his or her heart and marriage to all that is contained in this prayerful reflection will find freedom, guidance, and healing from Heaven and come to know personally the power of Jesus and the Woman who "has already crushed his head."

May God, in His mercy, make it so.

Through the triumph of the Immaculate Heart,

—Dan and Stephanie Burke
Co-hosts of Divine Intimacy Radio & Marriage Retreats
SpiritualDirection.com

God's Plan for Your Marriage

Introduction

The family is the foundation of both the Church and society. Marriage is the foundation of the family. This means that the stability of the family, the Church, and society are dependent on the stability of the marriage. Indeed, we can say: "As goes the family, so goes the society." Thankfully, throughout the history of the Church, marriage has been steady and stable — the rock on which everything else could depend and on which they could stand firm. This is no longer the case.

In our day, marriage and the family have been attacked unmercifully and from many fronts. We regularly see attempts to redefine both marriage and family in order to make them something other than what God intended from the beginning. Pope St. John Paul II recognized the problems facing marriage and family life, and in 1981, he founded the Institute for Studies on Marriage and Family. He appointed Fr. Carlo Caffarra (later Cardinal Caffarra) to head this initiative. The first few years were very difficult for the institute. Since it was under the patronage of Our Lady of Fatima, Fr. Caffarra wrote to Sr. Lucia dos Santos, a Carmelite nun in Coimbra,

Portugal, who had seen the Blessed Virgin Mary at Fatima in 1917. He wrote simply to ask her prayers for the institute.

To his surprise, Sr. Lucia wrote back to him. Her letter (written in 1983 or 1984) ended with these words: "Father, a time will come when the decisive battle between the Kingdom of Christ and Satan will be over marriage and the family. And those who work for the good of the family will experience persecution and tribulation. But do not be afraid, because our Lady has already crushed his head."

Nearly forty years have passed since these words were written, but this distance in time allows us to see clearly the prophetic nature of these words. Throughout the history of the Church, the devil has never ceased to attack and attempt to undermine the truth and, therefore, the stability of the Church. The attack on marriage and the family, however, is the worst and most evil plot the devil has devised. The effects on the lives of the spouses and their children are incalculable; the effects on the Church and society are aimed at their total demise. Thankfully, we have the promise of our Lord that the gates of Hell will not prevail against the Church, but this does not mean the forces of evil will not be able to inflict deep and profound wounds in the Bride of Christ.

History grants us the insight to know there are two things of which we can be assured in the aftermath of every diabolical attack. First, the area attacked will be stronger in the end. God brings good out of evil, so marriage and the family will be built up and strengthened — or better, purified and perfected like gold tested in fire. Second, God will raise up people to write, teach, defend, and develop the doctrines of the Church regarding the area under attack. He raises up men, women, and children whom no one would ever expect, and they become catalysts to implement the teachings of the Church and to provide new insights and further the development of doctrine.

It must be understood from the outset that this book is not intended as a practical guide to marriage. There are a handful of practical points in this book, but we must remember that marriage is first and foremost a spiritual reality. There are four general areas into which married life can be broken: communicational, relational, physical, and spiritual. The spiritual aspect of marriage is the foundation for the other three areas, but if a couple were to go for marriage counseling, very rarely would anything be said about the spiritual part of the relationship. The other areas are all important, but since the foundation for the marriage is spiritual, it is necessary to make sure the foundation is in good shape before trying to repair the higher stories or the roof of the building.

Therefore, the focus of this book is on the spiritual dimensions that underlie the beautiful union of husband and wife as well as the expression of that union. The sacrament of Holy Matrimony is a spiritual reality. However, because it is lived on the natural, worldly, or material plane, it is very easy to forget the dignity and beauty of what God has made. The purpose of this book is to help married couples to know and understand the dignity and beauty to which they have been called and to provide some insights to help them to live their sacrament in a spiritual way.

Each person is made in the image and likeness of God. Marriage presupposes this truth and builds upon it. This means that married life conforms to the will of God and therefore directs those called to this lofty vocation toward becoming saints. The saints had to live in this world, but they always did so with their focus on God. They served the people around them with the love they had received from God. This summarizes the way of married life and love.

I had intended to write a book for couples preparing for marriage, yet this book is almost entirely directed at married couples. There are two reasons for this. First, the contents of this book will be very informative for people who are married. It is my assumption that the majority of the people who will read this book are already married. Second, many couples preparing for marriage are so distracted by all the other preparations they need to make that they often do not take the spiritual formation seriously. Even the presentations on relational and intimacy issues tend to go in one ear and out the other. With this in mind, the book will be more useful for these couples a few years after they are married, when they are struggling and actually want something that will help them.

The chapters are broken down as follows:

"From the Beginning": The book begins with the accounts of creation in the first two chapters of Genesis and considers the dignity of the human person and our common call as persons made in the image and likeness of God. It provides insight into the Fall of our first parents and the effects their sin has had on the rest of humanity. It also looks at the strengths and weaknesses inherent in us as males and females and discusses how, like Adam and Eve, we will each be tested in our love for and fidelity to the Lord.

"God Is Love": After the Fall of Adam and Eve, almost everything changed, but God's intention for humanity remained the same. With their dignity still intact, the first human persons, and everyone after them, retained the ability to live according to truth, love, and life. This chapter considers love and what it means in our relationships with God and with one another. Moreover, it applies these principles to marriage and what they require of couples in their marital relationship.

"What God Has Joined": Love given and received brings about a union of persons. This union is expressed most profoundly in the vocation to marriage. Marriage can be natural or sacramental, and this chapter presents the differences in the kind of union experienced in each. Covenants are also discussed because sacramental marriages are also covenants the couple enters into with each other and with God. This leads to what is required for the sacrament of Holy Matrimony to be valid or invalid.

"The New Creation": Marriage, being one of the few aspects of human life that survived the Fall, has now been raised to a new level by our Lord. Jesus came into this world to reverse the devastation caused by sin and to provide us with a new start. He did not restore everything as it was before the Fall, but He has given us the means to live as God created us to live. We now have the choice to live as a new creation or to remain in the fallen order. The marital relationship, in a particular way, provides the means to overcome the effects of Original Sin if the couple is willing to embrace their call, to work to overcome their natural weaknesses, and to live according to their redeemed manhood and redeemed womanhood.

"*Consummatum Est*": Because marriage is first and foremost a spiritual union, a married couple must strive to develop a prayer life. The more they love God, they more they will love one another, and the deeper their union will grow. That spiritual union is expressed physically in and through the body. Within the sacrament of Holy Matrimony, this expression of love is not merely physical; it is the giving and receiving of the whole person; it is holy. This leads into a discussion of the necessity of serving the needs of the other and of protecting the relationship from sin and selfishness.

"You Are the Temple": Marriage, St. Paul tells us, is a mystery that reflects the union of Christ and His Bride, the Church. Beginning with the relationship between Jesus and His Bride, this chapter considers the spiritual union of the married couple. St. Paul also tells us we are temples of the Holy Spirit. How this applies to a couple in marriage is a focal point in understanding the holiness of the union of souls. This holiness has Baptism as its foundation, as each baptized person is a member of Jesus Christ and shares in His threefold office of priest, prophet, and king. Each of these offices is considered in the context of the marital relationship.

"The Banquet of the Lamb": The holiness and love within a marriage require a dying to self in order to live for the other. This truth is considered in light of the sacrifice of Jesus. This leads to looking at some of the correlations between the Holy Eucharist and marriage and, further, to the connections between marriage and Heaven. Holy Matrimony is a preparation and foreshadowing of Heaven, the marriage banquet of the Lamb.

1

From the Beginning

"From the beginning." This is a phrase we are accustomed to hearing during musical and theatrical rehearsals, indicating that everyone should go to the start of the movement or the beginning of the piece. It is important to our considerations because Jesus Himself uses the phrase "from the beginning" to tell us that if we want to know God's will regarding marriage, we need to go back to the start. To be more specific, we are told in the Gospels of Matthew and Mark that some Pharisees came to Jesus and, to test Him, asked if a man could divorce his wife for any reason. When Jesus asked what Moses allowed, the Pharisees answered that Moses allowed a man to divorce his wife. Jesus replied that it was because of the hardness of our human hearts that Moses allowed this, but it was not God's will "from the beginning" (Matt. 19:3–19; Mark 10:2–12).

The phrase "from the beginning," or similarly, "in the beginning," is used thirty-five times in Scripture to refer either to the time when God began His work of creation (and the time shortly thereafter) or to the period that preceded creation, when God alone existed. For the purposes of our considerations, the phrase also applies to the beginning of a marriage because, as we will see, this union denotes a new creation.

Before we can consider marriage in Christ as the new creation, we must ask what God's original intention is for those called to this holy state in life. God cannot change; therefore, His intentions regarding marriage have not changed. This is why Jesus refers us back to the Garden of Eden: that is where God first revealed His intentions for married life. So, as it is with the musicians from our example, we have to go back to the beginning, to the time when God began creating, to the beauty and glory of the human persons created in God's image and likeness, and to that brief time of bliss, that blessed time when the first couple was married.

We are told that on the first day of creation, God separated the light from the darkness (Gen. 1:3). This confuses a lot of people because the sun was not created until the fourth day. Scripture speaks not about a physical light on the first day, however, but about a *spiritual* light and darkness. The angels were created outside of time before God began His material creation, so it was on the "first day" that God created the angels. Before the angels could enter Heaven, however, they had to pass a test. From what can be ascertained, the angels were asked to accept God's plan for the salvation of creation. Some angels rejected this or that truth, but the most common stumbling block seems to have been with Jesus and Mary. The angels were shown a Baby; they knew the Baby was God, but why would God lower Himself to take on the nature of a creature infinitely lower than Himself and even lower than the angels? They were also shown a woman who loved God so much that she would be elevated higher than the angels. She would be the Mother of God, and she would be the angels' queen. How could a human person, whose nature is lower than the nature of the angels, become higher than the angels? From a rational perspective, this made no sense.

Angels are persons; this mean they are living beings who have minds and free wills. The angels were asked to make an act of faith regarding a mystery that surpassed their ability to understand. Those angels who accepted God's plan entered immediately into Heaven, into the light of truth and love. Those angels who rejected God's plan chose darkness and removed themselves from all possibility of light. The angels had only one chance to accept God's plan because angels choose with their whole being; therefore, they cannot change their minds. This seems unfair to us because we have many opportunities to repent and try again. We must understand that the angels had full knowledge both of what they were choosing and the consequences that would follow from their choice.

When Satan and those who chose to be in league with him refused to accept God's plan, it was not only an act of pride and disobedience. They rejected God, who is truth, love, and life. Satan stated: "I will not serve." Service is the expression of love, and love is an act of the will, so Satan used his will to choose against love. He chose to be selfish. In choosing against truth and love, the devil also chose death over life because he lost sanctifying grace, which is the life of God. So we see there were two possibilities for the angels: they could choose truth, love, and life; or they could choose a lie, selfishness, and death.

Likewise, every person has to be tested to determine whether he or she will choose God and His ways. What we have already seen tells us that we will be tested, not only regarding Jesus and Mary and the other mysteries of our Faith but also regarding truth, love, and life. Sometimes the teachings of the Church regarding marriage do not make sense to a couple. Will they accept the

Church's teachings and conform themselves to the truth in love? Or will they choose a different way, a way different from what God has revealed as His plan for married life and love? Will they, like Satan, reject God's way and try to establish their own ways?

You may have noticed that I started with the third verse of Genesis instead of the first or second verse. I did this because the creation of the human person can be understood only in the light of God. In the first verse, we hear about God creating the heavens and the earth. In the second verse, the Spirit of God is hovering over the waters. Since we know that God is a Trinity of Persons, we will begin with that assumption. In Genesis 1:2, the Spirit is divine, but He is specifically called the "Spirit of God," which implies that He is not the Father. Couple this with what we read in the first verse of St. John's Gospel: "In the beginning was the Word, and the Word was with God, and the Word was God." Once again, we notice that if the Word, who is God, was with God, He is not the Father either. Now we see references to three Divine Persons: the Father, who is simply known as God; the Word; and the Spirit. All three are God, all three are equal, and all three are eternal. This means that the Word and the Holy Spirit were not created. Being eternal, the Word and the Holy Spirit have no beginning and will have no end.

In Genesis, it is not possible to show the Trinity of Persons in the unity of one God, but there is clear reference to this truth. God is called *Elohim* in the first chapter of Genesis. The word *Elohim* is plural, yet it is translated only in the singular: "God," not "Gods." Moreover, if anyone thinks this is a mistranslation, note that this chapter uses a verb in the third person singular every time it mentions God's naming something. When we translate these words into English, we would use a pronoun that is properly translated in the singular as well. For instance, "He called the darkness night"

(Gen. 1:5). The pronoun "He" is singular. There is only one God, but He is referred to as a plurality of Persons.

Persons, as we have seen, are living beings with minds and free wills. Because there is only one divine nature, there is only one divine mind and one divine will, which are equally shared among the three Persons who are God. Consequently, there are three Persons who know (mind) and love (will) one another perfectly. It is this perfect knowledge and perfect love that form a perfect unity among the Persons of the Trinity. This also shows the relational nature of God, which goes beyond the three Persons of the Trinity and extends to rational creatures who are made to share in His truth, His love, and His life.

In Creation, God's first act was to create persons, angelic persons, who are pure spirit. His last act was also to create persons, human persons who are made of both body and spirit. Between these two acts of creation was a series of creative acts that build upon and perfect one another. Thus, there is a correlation between what happened on the first and the fourth days, the second and the fifth days, and the third and the sixth days. There is also a growth of perfection in material creation. The angels, having no bodies, are not part of material creation. Within the creation of material things, God begins with the inanimate and works toward the animate. Among the animate creatures, He begins with the lesser and moves toward the greater.

This growth in perfection is not simply a movement from the lesser to the greater. We saw in the second verse of Genesis that the Spirit of God hovered over the waters. For the ancient Hebrew people, water was a sign of chaos because they could not control water. God's creation brings order into the chaos. As creation becomes more perfect, the order becomes greater and the chaos becomes less.

Each day of creation (the second day being an exception) ends the same way: God looks at what He has made and sees that it is good. The sixth day, however, reveals something entirely different. God creates the animals on the sixth day and then stops, looks at what He made, and sees that it is good. This is the only day He stops halfway through the day! There is a very profound reason for this: to call attention to what He is going to do next; to show that the creatures He would create in the second half of the sixth day are entirely different from anything else He created and that these creatures would cause a substantial shift in the whole of creation.

In the creation of everything in the first five and a half days, God simply determines to make whatever He wills. As the psalmist says: "[God] spoke, and it came to be" (Ps. 33:9). Each day we are told, "God said," and it was made. Embarking on the pinnacle of His creation, God does something He has not yet done. He says, "Let us make man in our own image, after our likeness" (Gen. 1:26). "Let us" is a reference to the plurality of Persons in the Trinity, but it is also a reference to the relational aspect of God and to the fact that He has chosen to make persons in His own image and likeness. Nothing else in material creation is a person; nothing else has a mind and a free will.

God has also created us male and female. In other words, both male and female are equal, as in the Trinity, in which there are three distinct Persons but all are equal. In creating human persons, the Lord not only made us equal and distinct but made us unique individuals. We will discuss some of the differences between males and females in a later chapter, but these differences do not make us unequal. Our abilities are not equal, but as persons we are absolutely equal.

Each of us has a human soul. The human soul is neither male nor female; it is created by God to inform a male or a female body.

The soul has two faculties: a mind and a free will. The mind is made for truth, the will is made for love, and the soul is the principle of life. Therefore, the human person is created for truth, love, and life—to live in relationship with the Trinity. God made us to share in His life, and this means we are also to know His truth and live in His love.

This begins to unlock for us the mystery of our dignity as human persons. What a gift to be a person! What an amazing gift to be made in the image and likeness of God! But it gets better. In Genesis 1:31, we read something even more astounding. As we saw earlier, God stopped halfway through the sixth day and looked at what He had made and found it all to be good. Then He made us in His own image and likeness, and, as He had done on the other days, He looked at what He had made, and He saw that it was *very* good. In the original Hebrew, this would have an exclamation point after it. God looked at what He had made and, indeed, it was very good!

In creation, everything is declared good, and only one thing is declared very good: the human person. This is your dignity! This is who you are! This does not mean everything you do is good, but it does mean your nature is very good. A point needs to be made here that cannot be overemphasized: human nature cannot change. Your nature cannot change. People can violate your dignity. In fact, you can violate your own dignity. But nothing and no one can diminish your dignity even in the smallest degree.

It is critical that we understand this point. Our nature is very good, and our dignity is immense. This cannot change, regardless of how badly we may be violated or may violate ourselves. This understanding of human nature is the primary difference between Catholics and Protestants. Martin Luther taught that when Adam and Eve fell, their nature was corrupted. As Catholics, we believe that our nature was wounded but not corrupted. If something is corrupted, it is no longer what it was before. It has changed into something else. Think of the consequences. If your nature has been corrupted, you can have no part in salvation, because Jesus took on a human nature to save those who have a human nature. If your nature has been corrupted and is no longer a human nature, then you can have no part in Jesus or anything that follows from our union with Him.

Consider this: our nature is so good that the Son of God took on our human nature, and it was not offensive to Him. Rather, He raised us, with our human nature, to a divine level of acting and being. He did not take on a corrupted nature, because then He would not be true man. He is true God and true man, one Person with two natures.

If there is still doubt, another truth may help to clarify the point. When Satan fell, his nature did not change. He was created with an angelic nature, and he still has that same nature. Satan's nature is good. His will is perverted against God, but his nature remains unchanged. If Satan's nature was not corrupted when he fell, and his fall was substantially worse than the Fall of our first parents, then it should be clear that our nature was not corrupted either. No, our nature is still made in the image and likeness of God, and it is still very good. This cannot change!

Our society has done a superb job of denying the goodness of human nature and our dignity as human persons created in the image and likeness of God. Many people define themselves according to their sinfulness. This is not how God sees us, and it is not the way we should see ourselves. What is really sad is how willingly we listen to the devil's lies and how difficult we find it to believe God's truth. It is time to stop listening to the one who hates us and wants our destruction and, instead, to listen to God, who loves us and wants only what is best for us. Reject the lies and accept the truth! The difficulty we have with accepting the truth demonstrates how profoundly we have been wounded by sin, original as well as our own. Once we recognize our woundedness, we can turn to the Lord, seek His truth and love, and ask for His healing grace.

Love, by its nature, knows no bounds. It overflows any boundaries we can try to put on it. Of course, God is infinite, so with God there are no boundaries. His love is so great (as a matter of fact, it is infinite) that He wanted to share that love with rational creatures—that is, with creatures who could receive His love and could love Him in return. We cannot love what we do not know, so God wills to give us knowledge of Himself. God will never force us to do anything, so He offers us the grace to enter into a relationship with Him. The deeper we go in this relationship, the more we come to know the Lord. The more we know God, the more we can love Him. The more we love Him, the more we will want to serve Him.

What all this means is that we were made to know, love, and serve God in this life. God also chooses to share His life with us, so He offers eternal life to those who love Him and invites us into the fullness of truth, life, and love in the Trinity. None of this is an affront to our dignity. Rather, it is the fulfillment of our dignity. Because we are made in the image and likeness of God, we are made to be relational, as the Persons of the Trinity are relational. Each Person in the Trinity knows and loves the other Persons, but God also knows, loves, and serves each person He has created in His image and likeness. Each human person, created in the image and likeness of God, is made to know, love, and serve God and one another. This achieves perfection in the created order in marriage, in which the spouses know, love, and serve each other. Just as God reveals Himself to us so we can know Him and love

Him more, so spouses reveal themselves to each other in order that they may know and love each other.

The more we know about someone, the more we can love that person; the more we love someone, the more we will serve that person. This is true in regard to both God and other persons, especially one's spouse.

When we move into the second chapter of Genesis, another shift occurs. The first chapter can be understood as an objective perspective of creation, looking at creation from the outside and painting it in broad strokes. The second chapter presents creation from the subjective perspective: the perspective of the human person. It is almost as if we are able to look at things through Adam's eyes.

The second chapter is also marked by a shift in the way God is presented. In the first chapter, God is always mentioned in the objective sense. He is *Elohim*. Now, in the second chapter, God's proper name is revealed. In this chapter, He is always called *YHWH Elohim*. *YHWH* is the name God revealed to Moses (Exod. 3:14) and a name the Jewish people would never speak lest they say God's Name with even the slightest irreverence. Consequently, whenever *YHWH* is written in Scripture, the Jewish people pronounce *Adonai*, or "Lord." For this reason, in most translations, *YHWH* is translated as "LORD."

While there are many aspects of this second account of Creation that are fascinating, for our purposes we need to look at only a few points. The first is the creation of the man. The Lord God made the man from the dust of the earth. At this point there was a body for the man, but there was no life in him. Then the Lord God breathed the breath of life into the man's nostrils and the man became a living being. The soul, as we have seen, is the principle of life in a living being, so the man's body is made of the elements of the earth, but his soul is infused into him by God. The soul of the man is not divine; it is a natural part of the man. The soul gives natural life to the body, but it can also receive supernatural life, God's life, which is sanctifying grace. Since there had been no sin, we can assume Adam was created with sanctifying grace in his soul.

The Lord God then plants a garden in Eden into which He places all the birds and animals He formed from the same ground from which Adam was made. The bodies are similar in their organic composition, but the souls are entirely different. Animals do not have personal or rational souls; out of all creation, only human persons have a rational soul. Before creating the animals, however, God made all the plants spring up with two trees in the midst of the garden: the Tree of Life and the Tree of the Knowledge of Good and Evil. The trees are made, and Adam is given permission to eat the fruit of any of the trees in the garden except the Tree of the Knowledge of Good and Evil. This command would provide the test of the man's fidelity to God.

After God has Adam name all the animals, the man realizes that he is the only person in material creation. As beautiful as the animals are, none of them can fulfill the purpose of the man's creation. The man was created in the image and likeness of God; the animals were not. The man was created to be in a relationship of truth, love, and life with another person, but the animals are not persons. One can talk to an animal, but one cannot be in a relationship of true love with an animal because animals are incapable of such a relationship. We will address this point further in the chapter on love.

Being alone is critical for Adam. He can love the Lord God and be loved by Him, and this would fulfill the spiritual longing of his soul, but he also has a body, which seeks a physical expression of love and unity. God's love is life-giving in Adam and in everything around him; therefore, Adam's love needs to be life-giving if he is to fulfill his purpose of being like God. Somehow it is necessary for Adam to share in the creative work of God, which is the fruit of love.

Adam now understands in a very practical way that he is made not only for God but also for someone else. He has a body that participates in the image and likeness of God, but he lacks the means to express that image and likeness in a fully human way.

So God puts Adam into a deep sleep—a dying of sorts—in order to give life to the woman. The woman receives life from the man and then gives it back. This is the nature of true love, wherein both persons give and receive. This event in the garden serves as the pattern for the marital relationship, as we will examine later.

We have to consider for a moment what God did in making the last of His creatures. He took a rib from the man and built it into a woman. The rib is not a vital organ in the body. Rather, it is at the service of the most important organs, the heart and the lungs, which we normally equate with love and with life. To serve is to love, so in taking a rib from the man, God used a part of the man that was already at the service of love. God took that which was closest to the man's heart and built it into the person whom Adam would love and who would love him. The rib also points to the different roles of the man and the woman. Adam was told by God that he was to guard the garden (Gen. 2:15). Being a protector is part and parcel of being a man.

Some may take umbrage at the idea of a woman being protected by a man, but we have to remember that in the Song of Songs, the bride is called a garden enclosed (see 4:12). This points to the way a woman processes and experiences life in general. She takes things into herself and works them through from the inside. A man, on the other hand, keeps things at an arm's distance and tries to deal with them from outside himself. What this means is that, by nature, a woman is vulnerable; her husband is expected to protect that vulnerability. This is not to be understood as being in any way negative. On the contrary, it is this vulnerability that allows the woman to love as she does and, in particular, to be the best spouse and mother she can be. If she does not feel safe, she cannot let her guard down and allow herself to be vulnerable. The woman herself suffers loss from this, but the people around her, especially her husband and children, are bereft of the best she can give them. A man, by nature, is not as vulnerable, but just as the rib protects the heart, so is the man close to the heart of his wife, and he is therefore able to be vulnerable with her.

When Adam is awakened from his sleep, he realizes very quickly that something inside is different. He is missing something he had possessed prior to being put into the deep sleep. God could have made Eve from the dirt, as He had made Adam. He did not need to take the rib from Adam. Taking the rib from Adam to make Eve establishes the pattern of giving and receiving in the human relationship of love. We must be clear that Adam does not lose anything from his soul, and Eve is not lacking anything in her soul. Each has a soul that is fully human.

This is the context that allows us to understand the immense joy Adam expresses when he sees Eve. So important is this moment that we read the first recorded words of Adam: "This at last is bone of my bones and flesh of my flesh; she shall be called Woman, because she was taken out of Man" (Gen. 2:23). This is another human person, a person equal to himself. She is a person to whom he can give his love and from whom he can receive love. The love of God can fill the hearts of each person. They will each love God in return and then love each other with the love of God that has been given to them. This is the cycle of love for which they were both created. The woman is able to participate equally with the man in what God's wisdom determined only a human person is able to do: to express what it means to be a person—that is, to express knowledge and love in a physical or bodily way. Together they are able to fulfill everything it means to be made in the image and likeness of God. They can know and love each other, like the Trinity. They can be a unity of persons, like the Trinity. Their love can overflow and become life-giving like that of the Trinity.

As a couple, the man and woman are also able to participate in the creative work of the Trinity, allowing their love for each other to overflow the boundaries of the two and become life-giving for children. Adam recognizes the mystery of dying and rising to new life in the creation of his wife and in the union of the couple. He also realizes that the woman has the ability not only to give life back to him but also to receive life from him and conceive new life: the life of a child. In their mutual giving and receiving, God will continue His work of creating more human persons. Allowing God into their love will make their love life-giving for children: the man and woman providing the material for the child's body and God providing the soul. This is the reason Adam calls his wife Eve, meaning "life."

Because human persons are made to love and love overflows into life, God commands His human creatures to be fruitful and multiply (Gen. 1:28), as He had commanded all the creatures in the water, in the air, and on land to do (Gen. 1:22). This is the first commandment given to humanity, so it has a particular gravity. With this command, Adam and Eve are united in the marriage covenant. The man and woman understand that if they are going to be creative, like the Trinity, they must create in love. This way, new persons who are made to love and to be loved will be conceived in love and will be loved for themselves and not for any selfish reason.

This was the original disposition of the man and the woman, who were without shame because their love for one another was not tainted in any way by anything selfish.

Up to the point of Eve's creation, Adam is called *ha adam*, which means "the man." After Eve is created, he is no longer called *ha adam*, but *Adam*. Several references to him as *the man* are used when referring to him in relation to something or someone else, but now *Adam* becomes a proper name for the male person that corresponds with the proper name given to his wife.

We must address another critically important aspect regarding the creation of the woman. Recall what was mentioned earlier: in God's material creation as presented in the first chapter of Genesis, there is a growth in perfection. Each creature God made became more and more perfect, culminating with the creation of the human person. Looking at this from the perspective of the second chapter, however, we can now ask the question: Who was the last being created? The woman. If she was the last being God made, then it follows that she must also be the most perfect or the highest of all the material creatures in creation. Once again, we need to be careful because higher does not mean better or greater. Remember that both the man and the woman are radically equal because both possess a human soul.

God's creation is now complete. But just as the first persons He created (the angels) had to be tested, so, too, His human persons have to be tested. So God tells our first parents that they can eat of any of the trees in the garden, including the Tree of Life, but they are not to eat of the Tree of the Knowledge of Good and Evil.

Satan makes his way into the garden; this means that Adam had already failed in guarding the garden. Then Adam fails to protect his wife by allowing her to talk with the vile creature. The devil asks if God really said they could not eat of any of the trees in the garden, although he knows that only one tree is forbidden to them. Eve responds that they can eat the fruit of any of the trees, but regarding the tree in the middle of the garden, they could not eat it or even touch it, lest they die (Gen. 3:1–3).

Satan tells Eve that they will not die; by this, he implies that God is a liar. And he goes further, saying that God does not want His human creatures to eat the fruit because, upon eating it, they would become like God, knowing good and evil. Yet Adam and Eve were already made in the image and likeness of God! God is absolute goodness, and, as we have seen, humanity was very good. To eat the fruit of the Tree of the Knowledge of Good and Evil would give Adam and Eve knowledge of *evil* and make them like the evil one, who rejected God and His goodness. Still, this fruit that gave knowledge is attractive to the mind. The choice to be obedient or disobedient is the domain of the will. The fruit itself, which can be eaten, corresponds to the desires of the body. Eve picks the fruit and shares it with Adam, who follows his wife into sin. Like the devil and his minions, our first parents choose lies, selfishness, and death over truth, love, and life.

Sin, concupiscence (the intemperate desires of the flesh), and death came into the world due to the disobedience of our first parents. God had brought order out of chaos; Adam and Eve brought chaos into God's order. Like the fallen angels, they chose darkness over light. The darkening of the mind makes it more difficult to know the truth. The weakening of the will makes it more difficult to discern and choose the greatest good. The darkness of death affects both body and soul. The soul loses grace, and the body will lose natural life. Adam and Eve were created with the gifts of integrity to pass on to their children;

now all they could pass on was their humanity in its fallen and darkened state.

Satan rejected the truth. Each of us must ask: "Do I want the truth?" The truth can be hard, and, in his cunning, the enemy of our souls will present to us an easier way, a selfish way. Jesus told us to enter by the narrow gate that is at the end of a hard road (Matt. 7:13–14). This is difficult for people today because the objective truth is often not socially acceptable. There is a cost to living the truth: we will be ridiculed and rejected. As painful as that can be, if we choose the truth in love, we are choosing to conform ourselves to Jesus, who is the truth. Beyond that, we will be fulfilling the eighth beatitude, which pronounces blessed those who are persecuted and slandered for our Lord's sake (Matt. 5:11; Luke 6:22). We must remember our Lord's promise that we will know the truth and the truth will make us free (John 8:32). Lies and sins enslave us; the truth will set us free.

Satan rejected love. Each of us must ask: "Do I want to love?" We are made for love, but consider how badly sin has affected us. God had to come to Earth, command us to do the very thing we were created to do, and teach us how to do that. It is difficult to serve. It is difficult to die to oneself, which is why our society tells us to look out for "number one." But dying to oneself is what love is all about. Look at the Cross. Look at the creation of Eve. We see a dying to self in the loving service of another. This might look daunting, but it is the only way to your—my—true fulfillment as a person.

Satan rejected life. Each of us must ask: "Do I want life?" In a world that has rejected God, the only idea of life is in the here and now, and people seek the good life. "Good" in this context means not moral goodness but pleasure, wealth, and materialism. What the world, the flesh, and the devil have to offer is what brings spiritual death.

There is a battle raging for your soul. Think of how precious and valuable your soul must be if God would give His own Son to save it and Satan would do anything to destroy it. God offers you eternal life, and Satan offers eternal death. If it were simply the choice between Heaven and Hell, it would be easy, but the choice must be made daily. It is the choice we have seen over and over: truth or lies, love or selfishness.

Lies and selfishness culminate in death. Truth and love lead to life.

More than 3,500 years ago, Moses presented God's will to the people of Israel and placed before them life and death, the blessing and the curse. For each of us individually and for each married couple, the same choice is presented and placed before us today. God, as He did through Moses all those years ago, pleads with us now: "Choose life" (Deut. 30:19).

We are told that after Adam and Eve had fallen, the Lord God was walking through the garden. Perhaps our idea is that God was strolling through the garden, enjoying the beauty He had created. But the word used in Hebrew suggests that He was walking briskly and with a purpose. He wanted to be in a loving relationship with His human creatures, but now, like some of the angels, Adam and Eve had chosen against loving Him. What is worse, Adam and Eve chose against themselves, because they chose against the love for whom and for which they were created. They violated their relationship with God and lost His life in their souls. They had acted selfishly, and now they were plagued by that selfishness as they looked upon each other in a way that violated their dignity.

In their guilt and shame, Adam and Eve try to hide from God. Needless to say, this does not work. God asks Adam why he is hiding. Adam tells God he was afraid because he was naked.

God then asks Adam if he has eaten of the tree of which he was forbidden to eat. The exchange that follows is as frustrating as it is fascinating—both because human nature has not changed over the centuries and because any married couple will be able to see this pattern in their own relationship. Adam, rather than taking responsibility for his actions, immediately points the finger at Eve. "It was the woman you gave me," he says. When God asks Eve about what she has done, she immediately points the finger at the serpent who tricked her.

With the Fall, charity—the highest form of love—was lost to their souls. Humility, the correlative virtue of charity, was upstaged by pride. Pride does not want to admit fault; it is always someone else's fault. Actually, if you look closely at Adam's response, he blames God for the Fall. "It was the woman *you* gave me." Adam claims he would not have fallen if God had not given him this woman, for whom he was so grateful before. So Adam blames God, and Eve blames the devil, but the choice to eat the fruit was theirs, and so are the consequences of their choice.

God responds first by cursing the serpent. This is good for all of us, but the vile creature does not lose any of his intellectual capacity, so we still need to deal with a being who is exceedingly more intelligent and subtle than we are. The Lord God also tells the vile creature that there will be enmity between him and the woman, between his seed and hers. (Remember this fact because it will become important later.)

God then addresses Eve, who receives two punishments. The first is that she will experience pain in childbirth. The second is that the man will rule over the woman, but the woman's desire would be for the man. In other words, the relationship between men and women was turned upside down, for before, the man was to love his wife and his desire was to be for her. This punishment is given to the woman because she is relational by nature. Clearly, both the man and the woman are affected by problems in their relationship, but it is a much heavier burden for the woman.

Next, God curses the ground. Because of Adam, the soil will not bring forth the produce of its own accord but will bring forth thorns and thistles. Adam will have to obtain his food by the sweat of his brow. Beyond this, God tells Adam he will die and will return to the dirt from which he was taken. Needless to say, both the man and the woman will die; since the woman was taken from the man, if the man is to die, then the flesh taken from the man will die as well. So we have one punishment that affects each person directly and one that will affect them both.

Notice that the punishments have to do with two things: life and the origin of the persons. Adam was made from the ground; now the ground is cursed, and in order to sustain life, Adam will need to suffer. Eve was made from a living human person, so in order to give birth to a human person, she will need to suffer. So there would be hardship in the relationship between the man and the woman. There will be suffering in bringing new life into the world, and there will be suffering in sustaining life. And, at the end, humanity will have to suffer the sting of death. Death came as a result of the choice of our first parents, but Scripture tells us that death entered the world through the devil's envy (Wisd. 2:24). Envy is the anger one feels at the good fortune of another. Satan was filled with envy because Adam and Eve possessed what he rejected. In his hatred, he wanted to deprive them of the truth, love, and life he rejected.

One final point that is of critical importance for us: the humans were not cursed. Satan was cursed, and the ground was cursed; Adam and Eve were not. This means we all have to deal with the effects of Original Sin, but we are not cursed. The Lord God still loves us and still wants to be in relationship with us. He invites us into the love of the Trinity, and He desires to be invited into the love of each person's heart and into the love of each married couple. This is the choice God has made. Now we have to make our choice: to live the truth in love or selfishly to embrace a lie that leads to death.

Questions for Reflection

1. How does your love for your spouse reveal each Person of the Trinity's love for the other Persons? What about your spouse's love for you?

2. "To serve is to love." What more could you do to show your spouse love by serving him or her?

3. If you're a man, how does Genesis 1 speak to your nature *as a man*? How are you like Adam? If you're a woman, how does Genesis 1 speak to your nature *as a woman*? How are you like Eve?

4. Adam and Eve "rejected God and His goodness." How can your family be open to Him, like St. Joseph and our Lady? How can you "choose life"?

2

God Is Love

When God began His work of creation, everything was chaos. His creative work brought order out of the chaos. More to the point, His *love* brought order out of the chaos. As we've seen, there is an order of perfection in material creation. The summit of this creation was the human person, who was made to love and to be loved. Sadly, it did not take long for the first persons to fail in the very purpose of their creation by choosing to act selfishly rather than to act in charity.

Everything God created He made for His human creatures. His creation was characterized by order and harmony. For humanity, this was both internal and external. The two persons were at peace within themselves, they were at peace with one another, and they were at peace with the rest of creation. Most importantly, they were at peace with God, because they were united with Him and truly loved Him with their whole hearts, minds, and souls. The acceptance of Satan's lie that God did not want what was the best for them caused them to withdraw their hearts and minds from God and to focus on themselves. Their sin broke this communion with God and brought chaos into the created order. Once again, this chaos was both internal and external. All of nature is affected by the choices human beings make, whether they act in love or in sin. The more we love, the more orderly things will be within ourselves and with everything and everyone around us. The more we sin, the more the internal and external chaos grows.

When they were created, Adam and Eve had what is called "original integrity," meaning that their minds and their wills had complete mastery over their bodies and their senses. The choice to sin brought disorder into their minds and their wills. Confusion was introduced as their senses began demanding to be stimulated, and Adam and Eve lacked the ability to push aside any disordered desires easily. The relationship between the man and the woman became strained as they struggled to rein in selfish and unchari-table thoughts and desires that were directed toward each other, especially lust and domination. The disorder and chaos within and between Adam and Eve were so pervasive that the only things remaining were the dignity of their persons, the purpose of their creation, and the unity of their persons brought about through their marriage. Nothing else was the same.

When God tried the angels, the choice each one made resulted in that angel's entering the heavenly paradise or rejecting it forever. Our first parents also had a choice to make, and that choice would result in whether they would remain in the earthly paradise or reject it forever. Thankfully, the possibility of entering into the heavenly paradise is still open to us, even after the sin our first parents com-mitted and after all the sins we have personally committed. Adam and Eve were expelled from Eden because the chaos they chose was incompatible with the order God had created.

The expulsion of Adam and Eve from the earthly paradise was not a rejection by God of His human creatures. Nor, for that matter, was it a complete rejection of God by Adam and Eve. This is important because it meant that a relationship with God was still possible. It would not be the same as before they sinned, but they could still know, love, and serve God. Of course, He had not changed at all. His intention for His human creatures remained the same, as did His desire for a relationship with His human creatures.

It was mentioned earlier that everything God made, He made for humanity. However, He created humanity *for Himself*. Before we say more, we should be clear that God gets nothing from His creatures. He is absolutely perfect, and this means He lacks nothing. Nothing we can do adds anything to God; nothing we can give Him makes Him happier, more fulfilled, or more perfect. So to say we are made for God does not mean God made us for a self-serving purpose—so He could receive something from us. Just the opposite, in fact. Even our need for Him is a boon to us. Because we are made for love, the more we love God, the more we will be fulfilled. By knowing, loving, and serving the Lord, by following God's commandments, by praying, by striving to do God's will, we benefit. God does not.

It is still God's will to be in a loving relationship with us, but He will never force Himself on us. He created us with a free will and treats us as persons with a free will. In case there is any doubt in anyone's mind about God's intention toward us, we have to recall that God walked in the garden with Adam and Eve before the Fall and, as the use of the Lord's Name in the second chapter of Genesis would suggest, Adam and Eve enjoyed a very close relationship with Him. When the people of Israel had forgotten God—although He had not forgotten them or the covenant He had made with them—He revealed His Name to Moses on Mount Sinai (Exod. 3:14): the same Name, Lord, that is used in the second chapter of Genesis. In Proverbs, we are told about the personification of Wisdom, the Second Person of the Trinity, who says: "I was daily His delight, rejoicing before Him always, rejoicing in His inhabited world and delighting in the sons of men" (Prov. 8:30–31). Even more than this, God spoke through the prophet Isaiah, telling humanity that His Son would be born of a virgin and be called Emmanuel, "God with us" (see Isa. 7:14). St. Matthew quotes this same passage with regard to the birth of Jesus (Matt. 1:23). God is not just some distant being "out there." He is *with us* and finds His joy being among us.

More than anything, the Incarnation of Jesus and His Passion tell us of God's love for us. St. Paul tells us that God demonstrated His love for us in that, when we were still sinners, Christ died for us (Rom. 5:8). Many of us believe we are unlovable. At the very least, we say, "God cannot love me." For His part, God has done everything He can to prove His love for us. We should not require any proof because God told us of His love for us. Moreover, St. John states simply, "God is love" (1 John 4:8). In other words, even if we didn't have God Word, we know that His very nature is love.

This is pertinent to our considerations because it means the only way God can treat us is to love us. This is true because of His own being but also because of our humanity. Because we are made to love and to be loved, God will only love us. The problem, as we saw earlier, is that we were so badly injured by sin that we no longer knew how to love as we were created to love. Being made in the image and likeness of God tells us that if we want to know who we are to be and how we are to act, we first need to know God, in whose image and likeness we are created. Although God gave humanity many ways to seek and find Him, and to know and love Him, most people were unable to achieve union of love with God. And so, because we can find fulfillment only in being who we were created to be, God, in His love for us, chose to become one of us to teach us by His words and example how to love, how to receive love, what it means to love, what it means to be human, and what it means to be persons made in the image and likeness of God.

St. Paul called Jesus "the image of the invisible God" (Col. 1:15). Jesus is both God and man, so, in the unity of one Person, Jesus is able to show us through His humanity how God acts in truth and in love. More than just teaching us how to act this way, our Lord invites us into a relationship with the Trinity once again. He has "canceled the bond" that stood between us and God (Col. 2:14). He has reconciled us to God while we were still enemies of God (Rom. 5:10). He has given us free access to Himself (Matt. 11:27) and to His Father (Eph. 2:18). The Holy Trinity—the Father, the Son, and the Holy Spirit—dwells in the heart of every person who is in the state of sanctifying grace. Moreover, Jesus remains among us in the Eucharist and gives Himself to us sacramentally in Holy Communion.

God wants to be in relationship with us, and we can only be who we were created to be when we are in relationship with Him. To enter into this relationship with God, we need to pray. Every person needs his or her own life of prayer alone with God. Families have an added duty to pray together. A married couple must pray together, and parents should pray with their children. Remember that marriage is first and foremost a spiritual union. Everything in marriage flows from this spiritual union with God.

By its nature, prayer will, little by little, conform us to God and form us into the persons God made us to be. To be more Godlike means to become more and more transformed into love, which is the basis of both human and married life. St. Paul speaks of this transformation, saying: "We are being changed into His likeness from one degree of glory to another" (2 Cor. 3:18). In a sacramental marriage, the couple asks God to perform what is essentially a miracle and to unite them. This brings the couple into a union that is analogous to that of the Trinity. In God, three Persons are united; in marriage, two human persons are united by God—a union of a man, a woman, and God.

As we have seen, the unity of the Trinity is one of truth, love, and life. If individual prayer conforms a person to God, then praying as a married couple will unite the couple by conforming their minds to truth, their hearts to love, and the union of their souls in a common life. This life will be both natural and supernatural: the sharing of a natural life together and the supernatural union in grace. The couple needs to grow in love with God and with each other. And as the spouses grow in their mutual love, there will naturally be a desire for that love to flow beyond the two of them.

In other words, as much as a couple may be in love, they will not be satisfied by each other. Their love, which gives life to each other, has to transcend the boundaries of their own relationship and become life-giving for others. The couple is created to love as God loves, which means they are privileged to participate in His creative work. Most often this is expressed in the procreation of children, but in situations where this is not possible, the couple may be able to express their creative love through adoption or service to others.

We have spoken a great deal about love, but we have not addressed the question of what love *is*. Needless to say, if the spouses, on the day of their marriage, make a vow to love, one would hope they know what they are vowing. In fact, precisely because of this vow, I would submit that love is the domain of married couples. Married people should be experts in love and about love. We are made for love, and we will be fulfilled only in love, yet most people do not know what love is.

I used to ask the couples who came to my parish for marriage preparation why they wanted to get married. Almost universally, the answer was "Because we are in love." This is certainly an excellent answer, but I would always ask them what that means. The response was often something such as "It is the warm [or wonderful] feeling we have when we are together." I heard this so many times that I stopped asking the question.

When I speak with middle school children and the topic of love comes up, I ask them to think about the person in this world they love the most, suggesting that, for most of them, it will be either their mom or their dad. Then I ask them: "When you go home from school today and see your mom, are you going to have warm, gushy feelings about her?" They usually think that is gross. So I point out that love is clearly not a feeling. I go on to explain to them that they may sometimes have very bad feelings about their moms. In a fit of anger, they may even cry, "You're the worst mother ever!" And yet, as angry as they might be, they still love their mom. So there are emotions that come with love, but love is not an emotion.

If we look at the nature of love, we will find there are four characteristics that are necessary for love to be authentic. Each characteristic builds upon the previous characteristics. First, love is benevolent. *Benevolence* means "goodwill," so benevolence desires the good of the other. The second characteristic of love is that it is reciprocal. In other words, it requires two to love. To be in love with yourself is narcissism, and narcissism is a sin. It's pure selfishness. So, for love to be authentic, it requires two persons who have good will toward each other. This implies that neither is selfish when it comes to the other. The third characteristic of love is communion. The reciprocal benevolence of the two creates a communion of persons. The foundation of this reciprocal, benevolent communion is a fundamental similarity, which is the fourth characteristic of charity. What this means is that you cannot have a true relationship of love with something that is not a person. You can love your dog, but there is no fundamental similarity between a person and a dog. Moreover, the dog can emote toward you, but the dog is not capable of freely choosing to love you with an act of the will based on knowledge.

One might wonder how we can have a relationship with God since we lack a fundamental similarity. The answer is sanctifying grace. Grace is God's life in us, and it raises us to a supernatural level of acting and of being. It provides the fundamental similarity for our relationship with God. We know that God has only benevolence toward us, but for this love to be reciprocal, we must have benevolence toward God. The more perfect the benevolent reciprocity, the more perfect the communion of persons. This is true both with God and with others—and especially between spouses.

Love is an act of the will based on what we know. It is a choice. It means doing always what is best for the other. This means that our emotions and our circumstances should not affect what we choose to do toward another, because love always chooses to serve the other and always seeks the best for that person. When we say that love is doing always what is the best for the other, we must add that doing the best is not always the easiest, not always the most convenient, and not always what the other person wants. The stereotypical example of this is when a young man pressures a young woman for sexual favors while they're still dating. He says to her: "If you love me, you would do this for me." But if *he* really loved *her*, he would never ask her to do anything that would violate her dignity or his own. Looking at this from the perspective of the woman, if she gives in to the pressure, she sins against the young man and against herself. If she refuses the advances, she proves her love for him because she is doing what is truly best for him. St. Paul states the situation succinctly: "Love does no wrong to a neighbor" (Rom. 13:10).

Love is a virtue. In fact, St. Paul tells us love is the greatest virtue (1 Cor. 13:13). As English speakers, one of our challenges is that we lack the ability to distinguish different kinds of love without using adjectives to describe what we are talking about. To make the point, there are four Greek words for four types of love, all of which are translated into English simply as "love." So we can talk about the love of parents and children, or *storge*; we can talk about romantic or erotic love, or *eros*; we can talk about the love of friendship, or *philia*; and we can talk about unconditional love, or *agape*. In the New Testament, only *philia* and *agape* are used. They are used in both noun and verb forms. Unfortunately, no distinctions are made in the translations.

Perhaps the easiest way to clarify this point is to look at the well-known conversation in the Gospel of St. John between Jesus and Peter after our Lord had risen from the dead (21:15–17). Jesus asks Peter three times: "Do you love me?" Peter answers three times: "You know I love you." However, the first two times, Jesus asks: "Do you love [*agape*] me?" Both times Peter responds: "You know I love [*philia*] you." The third time Jesus asks: "Do you love [*philia*] me?" Peter responds the same way as before. Jesus is asking if Peter loves Him the way God loves or, perhaps better, if Peter loves Jesus the same way Jesus loves Peter. Peter is not yet able to love Jesus with *agape* love but can love Jesus only as a friend. In essence, our Lord goes on to explain to Peter that the day would come when Peter would be able to love with *agape* love (John 21:18). This is what St. Paul describes as being changed or transformed from one degree of glory to the next (2 Cor. 3:18).

This distinction is critical for us in our deliberations regarding married love because *agape* is the word that is always used for married love in the New Testament. The Latin word that corresponds to *agape* is *caritas* or *charity*. This is the love that is vowed on the day of marriage. Even the vows themselves attest to this truth. A couple does not vow to love "if," or "but," or even "as long as I feel as if my needs are being met," or "as long as I feel loved by you." No, the couple make a vow to love each other every day for the rest of their lives. Their vow is unconditional.

We will come back to the vows later in this chapter. First, we need to consider the nature of love in this highest sense—not only because this is the kind of love vowed in a marriage but because it is the kind of love Jesus requires of us when He tells us that the greatest commandments in the law are to love God and to love our neighbor (Luke 10:27). Our Lord also tells us we have to love our enemies (Matt. 5:44). Therefore, *philia* (friendly love) will not suffice. Only a divine kind of love will fulfill these commandments.

In marriage, the vow to love implies that two people have freely chosen to serve each other, to build each other up, to seek always and only the good of the other. In the most fundamental sense of this vow, doing what is best means helping each other to grow in holiness and to become saints. All too often, people think of marriage as a lesser vocation. Marriage is a call from God to a particular way of life designed specifically to make each of the spouses saints. The saints in the Church have served God in a variety of ways, but it was not the works they did that made them saints: it was their heroic love for God and neighbor.

By its very nature, love never remains the same. It either increases or decreases. No one loves his or her spouse the same today as yesterday. Professing the marriage vow requires the couple to increase their love for each other every day. In fact, if the day ever comes when you look at your spouse and think, "I do not love this person as much today as I did yesterday," you need to do some serious soul searching. It would be easy to blame your spouse for your diminished love, but remember that the vow to love is unconditional. If Mr. Smith doesn't love Mrs. Smith as much as he once did—if his love has not grown but has "shrunk"—then that is *his* fault, not hers. It may be true that your spouse is difficult to live with, but your love is not based on your spouse's behavior. Your love is your choice, and you must model it on the love of God. Jesus tells us that God makes His sun rise on the evil and on the good and sends the rain on the just and on the unjust (Matt. 5:45). Therefore, if Jesus tells us that we are to be like our Heavenly Father, you must love your spouse whether you think your spouse is loving as he or she has vowed to or not.

What if your spouse does not want to grow in love? If your spouse doesn't want to develop the marital relationship, then it is all the more necessary to pray for your spouse. Pray for your spouse's conversion or deeper conversion, pray for your marriage, but pray especially for the grace to love your spouse. If your spouse is not investing fully in the relationship, it's easy to justify yourself in treating your spouse the same way. But remember that our Lord expects us to treat others the way we want to be treated, not the way they treat us (Matt. 7:12). Remember the vow you have made to your spouse. You are not responsible for how your spouse lives his or her vows; however, you are accountable for how you live *your* vows. We saw earlier that love is to be reciprocal, but even when it is not, you can still make sure you are being benevolent toward your spouse. In the worst-case scenario, if you feel as if your spouse is your enemy or persecutor—as, unfortunately, many spouses feel—recall that Jesus told us to love our enemies and pray for our persecutors.

If you do not believe you are in love with your spouse anymore, begin asking God for the grace to fall in love with your spouse again, even if you feel that you do not want to be in love. And persevere in this prayer: it sometimes takes a year or more to change your own heart.

In some marriages, the love has faded away over the years. Even worse, the marriage may be marked by chaos. It may be that one or both spouses desire their marriage to improve, but they are afraid to upset the status quo, afraid to make the first step, or afraid of being rejected. In such a situation, there are two things to consider. First is the advice of St. John of the Cross that seems so obvious but manages to evade us in the fray. He said simply: "Where there is no love, put love, and there will be love." The second thing is to take the risk. Do not wait for your spouse to make the first move, because your spouse may be waiting for you. Again, remember the vow you made. Your vow is to love, even if your spouse is not loving as he or she vowed to you and to God.

Regardless of the circumstances in the marriage, a couple needs to pray for the grace of the sacrament every day. On the day of your marriage, God promised the sacramental grace for every situation that might arise in your marriage. However, God will not force anything on anyone. The grace is there, and God wants us to accept that grace, but He is waiting for the married persons to ask for it. So, whether your marriage is going well or poorly, or is in a transition, ask for the grace promised to you on the day of your marriage to help you in the present circumstances. Grace doesn't make it easy. Grace makes it possible.

It may come as a surprise to many people that their love must grow daily. Most of us—whether married or not—are content to remain at the same mediocre level of love. We are afraid to love more because love always involves a risk. It requires making oneself vulnerable to the other. Most couples settle into a comfortable routine. Opening themselves up to change or to something new or unfamiliar is very uncomfortable. The risk is that we could be hurt or rejected. It seems safer to stay where we are rather than risk rejection, but one cannot grow in love without taking that risk.

Married couples need also to be aware that it is easier to make one's body vulnerable than to make one's heart vulnerable. Some couples thwart the growth of their love (the spiritual aspect of their marriage) by attempting to focus more on the physical aspect of the marriage. Since the body expresses the person, focusing only on the physical will not make love grow. In fact, it will often do the opposite, because the spouses will feel they are being used rather than loved. The failure to risk going deeper in love could cause the love to stop growing.

St. John tells us, "Perfect love casts out fear" (1 John 4:18). A profound trust must exist between a husband and wife that one will not be used, violated, or exploited by the other if they make themselves vulnerable. This trust grows as the couple practices being vulnerable with each other. As each spouse realizes that he or she isn't being violated, that spouse will be willing to open up at a deeper level. When the person finally has absolute confidence in the love of the other, there will be no fear, and the heart can be open completely.

One thing that is universal in the lives of the saints is that the saints are never satisfied that they are loving enough. They always strive to love more. This is what needs to happen in a marriage as well. When things are difficult, our selfishness and the many hurts we have endured in life make us pull into ourselves rather than going out of ourselves in love.

On the day of marriage, the love between the couple seems great. When things are emotionally high, very little love is required.

It's when things are difficult, when the emotions are down, that the love in a relationship is proven. When one spouse is able to treat the other the same way on a bad day as on a good day, you know the love is real and deep. When one spouse feels like not even greeting the other and yet chooses to treat him or her with charity, that is when the love is growing the most. It does not feel good, but this is where love is proven, demonstrated, and deepened.

St. Peter Chrysologus said, "Love is unreasonable." This doesn't mean love is foolish or stupid. Rather, it means love is not rationed or measured. One mustn't think about whether a certain act of charity should be performed. One mustn't consider whether someone deserves to be treated better. Love is a gift, not a reward. None of us deserves to be loved because of anything we have done to earn or merit love. As we have seen, because we are made in the image and likeness of God (who is love), we are created to love and to be loved. God loves us because we are lovable; we are to love one another for the same reason.

With this in mind, every married person needs to ask himself or herself: "Why do I love my spouse?" Before reading on, think about your answer. If your answer has to do with what your spouse does for you, or with your spouse's abilities or attributes, then it is not love. In such a situation, you like what you are getting from your spouse, but you are not truly loving him or her. The only proper reason to love your spouse is that your spouse is who he or she is.

We are to love each person for who he or she is. This was God's intention in creating each person; it is the way God loves us; and it is the way we are to love one another. You can appreciate what a person gives you, but you should love that person only for himself or herself.

This call to love is a huge challenge for us. We saw that, in Original Sin, we hurt ourselves so badly that God had to become one of us and command us to do what we were created to do—that is, to love (John 15:17). In fact, St. John tells us this is the commandment we had from the beginning (1 John 2:7; 3:11). So we already have struggles due to Original Sin, but then we can add all the sins we have personally committed. Remember, every sin is an act of selfishness, and selfishness is the opposite of love. With every act of selfishness, we inhibit our capacity to love; with every act of charity, we expand our capacity to love. We come into this world as the most selfish little creatures. This is necessary for survival. But as we grow, we need to learn to overcome the selfishness. This is the entire goal of the Christian life: to rid ourselves of selfishness and to be filled with love for God and neighbor.

As if it is not hard enough to overcome our own propensity to selfishness, we live in a society that is almost totally self-centered. This makes it even more difficult to grow in love because society pulls us into greater selfishness and tells us that acting selfishly is acceptable. At the same time, if we are determined to grow in love, the extra effort required because of our environment will help us to become saints more quickly.

In one of the most frequently chosen readings for a wedding, St. Paul tells the Corinthians what love is and what love is not. He gives us fifteen characteristics of love (he is talking about *agape* love, or charity):

> Love is patient and kind; love is not jealous or boastful;
> it is not arrogant or rude. Love does not insist on its own
> way; it is not irritable or resentful; it does not rejoice in
> the wrong, but rejoices in the right. Love bears all things,
> believes all things, hopes all things, endures all things. Love
> never ends.... So faith, hope, love abide, these three; but
> the greatest of these is love. (1 Cor. 13:4–8, 13)

If we look at the negative characteristics mentioned here, we find we can organize them into two basic categories: pride and anger. Ultimately, however, they all flow from one source: pride. Jealousy, boasting, arrogance, rudeness, insisting on one's own way, and rejoicing in what is wrong are all part of pride. Another word for *pride* is *selfishness*. The traits that fall under anger—irritability and resentfulness—also stem from our pride. We most often get angry because things are not the way we think they ought to be or because someone did something we did not want him or her to do. These things make us angry, but the anger is due to our selfishness or pride.

Humility is the antidote to pride, and the saints tell us the real proof of humility is patience. When we let go of our own will and selfishness in a situation, we can see the link between humility and patience. Perhaps this is why patience is the first in the list of St. Paul's characteristics of charity.

So humility and charity are connected in an absolute and unbreakable manner. The height of our charity will be equal to the depth of our humility. Most people like the idea of having a great measure of charity, but they do not like the idea of a profound humility—not because they do not like humility but because of what is required to obtain humility. The only way to obtain humility is through humiliation, and most of us do not like to be humiliated. The progress made in charity makes the humiliations worth it, but, unfortunately, it takes a lot of humiliations to attain a little humility. When we read about Jesus or the saints, this is the pattern we see. The suffering of the saints strips them of selfishness and allows them to develop the greatest love precisely because they have developed the most profound humility.

When two people marry, they make a vow to love—to practice charity. In other words, they are telling one another and God that, from that day forward, they will strive never to be selfish again. Needless to say, no one expects them to be able to do this right away. The hope and the intention is that by the time God calls them home to eternal life, they will have perfected their love. They will be selfless. They will have true *agape* love, true charity, for each other and for God.

Married couples grow in holiness by obedience to the duties of their state in life, just as the saints did. Marriage is specifically designed to make spouses saints—that is, it is designed to help spouses die to self and live for others. The vow they make places upon them the requirement to seek out the greatest privilege we can have in this life: union with God and with one another. This union is one of love. Once again, it is imperative that spouses know what it means to love because how they lived their vow to love will comprise a major part of their judgment when they die. Married people must understand this: on the Day of Judgment, they will not be responsible for how well their spouses lived out their marriage vows; they will be responsible for how well *they themselves* lived out their marriage vows. Since the vow is to love, it is necessary to make the love grow every day. Love is a virtue, and like any other virtue, it grows only when it is tested. This is why God does not allow the emotional high to remain for very long after the wedding day and why it occurs seldom thereafter. God wants your love to grow, so He allows the majority of the spousal relationship to be routine or even difficult.

This truth regarding the vow to love versus selfishness has ramifications beyond Judgment Day. It will determine where we will spend eternity. There are only two places that are eternal: Heaven and Hell. Heaven is pure love, and there, everyone loves with a perfect love, for two reasons. First, everyone in Heaven will have been perfected, so they will be able to love only perfectly, to the fullness of their capacity. Second, St. Paul tells us we will understand fully even as we are fully understood (1 Cor. 13:12). This means that each person in Heaven looks at God and (according to his or her individual capacity) sees every other person as God sees that person. This, in turn, implies that we will know every person as perfectly as we are able and we will be known by each person as perfectly as each person is able to know us. Since we can love only what we know, if we have a perfect knowledge according to our capacity, we will have a perfect love according to that same capacity.

Scripture speaks of Heaven as a marriage banquet (Rev. 19:9), but, lest we think Heaven is just a big party and not a matter of loving and being loved, St. Paul says "the kingdom of God is not food and drink, but righteousness and peace and joy in the Holy Spirit" (Rom. 14:17). One who is righteous is holy and Godlike and, therefore, one in whom love is perfected. This is the essence of sanctity.

Hell, on the other hand, is pure selfishness. Everyone there is absolutely selfish. Every person in Hell hates every other person in Hell. Everyone looks out only for his own interests. Every person in Hell is trying to move ahead, but every other person is trying to pull them back so they can get ahead themselves. Consequently, no one moves ahead — ever. Furthermore, as you may have surmised, everyone in Heaven is vulnerable with everyone else. Everyone in Heaven is perfectly humble. On the other hand, everyone in Hell is closed and selfish. Everyone in Hell is perfected in pride.

This life is a preparation for eternity, so choose wisely how you live. God made marriage to make married people saints. As we'll see later, marriage is a foreshadowing of eternity. Whether it's an eternity in Heaven or in Hell depends on whether you choose humility or pride.

When we talk about God's allowing struggles in marriage, we might think we would be better off if God were not involved so directly. It would be wrong to think so, for several reasons. First of all, on your wedding day, you and your spouse asked God to work something of a miracle to join the two of you together. You and your spouse cannot do this yourselves, no matter how hard you try. There can be no Christian marriage without God. It isn't an option.

Second, you asked God to be at the center of your marriage. Don't leave Him out! Love originates in God, so it is essential to keep Him at the center of your own life and at the center of your marriage.

St. John tells us: "In this is love, not that we have loved God, but that He loved us" (1 John 4:10). We can't initiate love. We can only respond to it. God loves us first, and we receive His love and love Him in return. This opens our hearts to receive even more love, which God then pours into our hearts (Rom. 5:5). We receive this greater love and are able to love Him with more love than we had previously. Once our heart is open, God fills it to the fullness of our capacity. We can then pour out that love on others. So God loves us, we love God, and we love others with the love God has poured into us. Each time we love, we open our hearts to a greater capacity to receive more love and to love more. This cycle is intended to continue for our whole life. As long as we are alive, we have the ability to grow in love.

It should also be noted that suffering, if accepted and cooperated with, opens our hearts in two ways. First, it purifies our hearts of any selfishness or attachments. Second, it stretches or dilates our hearts, making them capable of receiving more love. The goal of marriage, according to the vows, is to have a perfect capacity to love. Once again, this can be accomplished only with the help of God's grace.

God is a gentleman. He will not force Himself into your relationship. Beyond that, He will enter into your relationship only to the extent you are willing to invite Him. God loves you and will never violate you. He wants you to know Him, to know yourself, and to know your spouse more and more perfectly because, as we have seen, we cannot love those whom we do not know. The more perfectly we know a person, the more perfectly we can love that person. To know someone more, we have to keep going deeper and deeper into the mystery of that person, who is made in the image and likeness of God. There is no end to the depth of this mystery. As long as you live, you can know and love your spouse more.

Remember also that marriage is first and foremost a spiritual union. It takes "three to get married," as Archbishop Fulton Sheen said. Keep God at the center of your marriage through prayer, which will bring you into a greater knowledge and love of God. The depth of your relationship with God will transfer to your marital relationship, so you and your spouse will continue to grow in knowledge and love of one another. I remember overhearing a conversation between two married men as they spoke about their relationships with their wives. One man said, "If you think having relations with your wife is intimate, try praying with her." Prayer will bring a greater spiritual union, which can then be expressed through a deeper physical union.

This may all sound like "pie in the sky" thinking, but God does not hold out for us an ideal that cannot be achieved. It is true that such a deep marital union cannot be achieved easily, and certainly not without His help, but to live married life the way it was intended from the beginning is absolutely possible. If it were not, Jesus would not have told us to go back to the beginning so we could understand God's intention for married life and married love. To live married life as God intended is possible only if God is integrally involved in the relationship. This is what He intended from the beginning, and, as Jesus said, "With God all things are possible" (Matt. 19:26).

We have seen that married life is to be a foreshadowing of Heaven, but that means it should also be Heaven on Earth. To see how this is so, let us go back to what is entailed in the vows. Considering the back-and-forth that has to occur in a marriage, many people think marriage is a 50-50 proposition. If that were true, marriage as God intended would not only be an unattainable ideal but would be bound to fail, without exception. Perhaps this is why more than half of marriages end in divorce today. Once again, it comes down to the selfishness of not putting oneself fully into the marriage.

Marriage is not a 50-50 proposition. Marriage is a 100-100 proposition. The vow is to love, and love is about giving and receiving. Taking or using is the opposite of love, because giving and receiving define love. In marriage, the gift that is given is the person, and the gift is given 100 percent. It's a total self-gift. That means when a couple gets married, each person gives himself or herself totally to the other person, who, in turn, receives the gift of that person 100 percent. This means there is nothing left of yourself to take back and there is nothing left of the other person to reject. You have given yourself away completely, and you have received completely the gift of your spouse. Each takes on the identity of and the responsibility for the other.

As another foretaste of what is to come, one can see in this giving and receiving that there is a death and a rising to new life that takes place. Each spouse dies as that spouse gives himself or herself to the other, and each spouse receives new life from the gift given by the other. Both must choose to make themselves entirely vulnerable to the other for this mutual, reciprocal self-giving and receiving to occur.

In marriage, then, we see a perfect fulfillment of our Lord's words: that there is no greater love than to lay down one's life for a friend and to do so freely (John 15:13; 10:18). Spouses freely, lovingly lay down their lives for the sake of the other. It may sound like the laying down of one's life as a martyr would be easier, but, as the old saying goes, before we can die the death of a martyr, we must live the life of a martyr.

Married life is this constant dying to self in order to live constantly for the other. This requires that spouses learn about each other so they can know each other's needs and determine how best to respond to those needs. The needs of males and females differ in many areas, yet men tend to treat their wives the way they treat other men, and women tend to treat their husbands the way they treat other women. Sometimes a couple will treat each other the way they would want to be treated by their spouse, but this does not necessarily meet the needs of the spouse.

It is imperative for you and your spouse to communicate your needs to each other, not selfishly but to help you both to know and love each other better. Unless your spouse knows you and your needs, he or she cannot love you according to your needs. Indeed, a married couple must strive to put St. Paul's advice into practice: "Outdo one another in showing honor" (Rom. 12:10).

The more a couple is willing to be faithful to what they vowed in marriage, the more they will realize just how beautiful married life can be. Recall that there was a void in creation until we were created to fill that void and that there is a void that remains until a couple is united in marriage. However, there are two other voids: the void within each person and the void within the marital relationship. These two voids can be filled only by love. God gives

Himself to each spouse both individually and as a couple, but a person who has been called to marriage must also find fulfillment in and through another human person. If the spouses continue to grow in truth and in love, they grow in their likeness to God. As they open themselves to God's love, they will love God and neighbor more and more, so the void will be continually filled. But if they fail to grow in truth and love, they will not be able to fill completely the void in creation that they have been created to fill. This is true for both the individual person and the two who have become one in the bond of marriage.

Of course, the other aspect of the void in creation that is filled by a married couple is the place dedicated to new persons. A married couple fills a void God reserved for them in creation, and they help to fill the void within each other, but they also contribute to the fulfillment of creation through the gift of children. It was mentioned earlier that love knows no boundaries, and therefore the love of a married couple must overflow the boundaries of their own relationship. This is the fundamental principle of all of creation. But God, in His love for us, has called married couples to participate in His work of creation. Nothing greater on the natural level can be granted to a person than to be given the gift of children.

Each human person is the "overflow" of the love of the three Persons of the Trinity. Each person is also intended by God to be the overflow of the love of his or her parents. Every child is made in the image and likeness of God and in the image and likeness of his or her parents. A child, then, is a living, tangible sign of the love of God and of the love of his or her parents. When parents look at their child, they should see a living form of the love they have for each other. When you look at your children, you should see in living form the love you have for your spouse and the love your spouse has for you. The same is true of God. When He looks at us, He sees His love in a living, human form. He sees His own image being reflected back to Him.

Because our topic for this book is married life and love, most of our effort will be focused on the couple and their relationship. However, it must be stated clearly that there are two ends of marriage. The first end, or purpose, of marriage is the procreation and education of children.

The second end of marriage is the unity of the couple. Today we often see the order reversed, but a stable relationship of love within a marriage is the only proper place for children to be conceived and raised. What is best for children is to have both parents married and loving each other.

If children are the overflow of love and the living image of the love of their parents, then it is necessary that each child should be conceived in love. The child is a person who is to be loved for himself or herself. Spouses must be careful not to make children into objects of their own desire. It is excellent that couples want to have children, but they have to be careful not to fall into the trap of thinking they have an absolute *right* to have children. By this I mean that children are not commodities. One mustn't desire a child for one's own sake. That would be selfishness. One must desire a child for the child's sake.

We do not have the right to do whatever is required to conceive a child. If a couple is infertile, they may choose to use treatment options that are morally acceptable. However, when testing or attempts at pregnancy cross the line into something sinful, then the desired child is being treated as an object. Along with this, the parents are also being treated as objects and are often asked to perform sinful acts in order to try to conceive new life. We must remember that life and love cannot be separated. The Church is clear in her condemnation of *in vitro* fertilization, surrogacy, and artificial insemination precisely because of the reasons just mentioned. To conceive a baby in a petri dish is not an act of love, nor is rejecting the unused fertilized eggs (aborting tiny human persons). Artificial insemination requires at least two acts that violate charity.

A child is to be conceived within the act of love. Given the earlier discussion on love, we can now better understand the kind of disposition a husband and wife should have when they approach each other. Of course, if a child is conceived outside of an act of love, the child is still made in the image and likeness of God, is still made to love and to be loved, and still has all the rights and dignity with which every other human person is endowed. Nothing is wrong with the conception of the child or with the child, but there was something wrong with the act that resulted in the conception of the child. If the act was not one of love, then it was either lacking integrity or was sinful.

If the couple loves each other, they want only the best for each other. Joined together in marital love, the two of them fill that void in creation with their love and want only what is best for their children. This desire begins with the first moment of a child's life and extends through the whole of that life. Married people need to be careful of a subtle trap in their desire to love their children. As we saw earlier, there is an order to love. Love must originate with God and then flow through us to others. Parents love their children immensely, and, of course, they want to love their children more. This sometimes results in an inversion in the cycle of love.

If you want to love your children more, love your spouse more. If you want to love your spouse more, love God more. God is the source of love, so the love flows from God, through your spouse, and to your children. The time you spend with each other is not the measure of the love you have for each other. As parents know, once their first child is born, they do not have nearly as much time together as they did before the baby was born. With each child, the amount of time the couple has alone together decreases. If their prayer life is maintained individually and as a couple, however, the time a couple has together will increase in quality—its love—even if it decreases in quantity.

We saw earlier that married life is the way of saints because it is all about love and service. Moreover, marriage is designed to help each person break his or her sinful tendencies. This is certainly true for the couple who have vowed to love each other, but children bring this necessity to an immediate and higher level. Although a spouse can do many things for himself or herself, little children cannot. So, in a moment of selfishness, a husband may not do something kind for his wife because she's capable of doing the task alone. When it comes to children, however, even if that husband does not feel like doing something for them because he is tired or frustrated, he knows they cannot take care of their own needs. He will have to die to self in order to care for them.

In marriage, because the couple has vowed to love, they should consider the disposition with which they do their various tasks and ask themselves, "How much love is there in what I am doing?" St. Thérèse of Lisieux can teach us much about this topic. She taught what she called her "Little Way" of doing ordinary things with extraordinary love. This is something every person is capable of doing, with God's help. Whether it's mowing the lawn, doing the dishes, sweeping the floor, putting kids to bed, cleaning up a mess, driving the kids to a function, whatever—all these things can be done either begrudgingly, out of a sense of duty, or they can be done out of love.

How does one sweep the floor out of love? Perhaps it's easier to imagine if one spouse offers to do this task for the other. The husband tries to relieve the wife's burden for her because he loves her.

Another way to consider this is to think about the care you might take in preparing for a special event for your spouse, perhaps a birthday or an anniversary. When we take the time to prepare the house, coordinate with the guests, buy the gifts, and make all the other little efforts that go into planning a party, it's all for one purpose: to show your spouse how much you love him or her. This same kind of love can be transferred to the day-to-day, routine events of life.

Think back to the early stages of your relationship. If it was fairly normal, there was almost nothing one of you would not do for the other (except sin, of course). When one is trying to impress the other, hardly anything seems too much to ask. Even in the earliest stages of a marriage, the emotions make it easier for the spouses to practice heroic charity toward each other. However, once a couple has settled into the routine of married life, even responding to simple, easy requests can seem to be too much, and the response is "Do it yourself."

If your marriage relationship has settled into a routine, then in order for your love to grow and become perfect, God is asking you to practice heroic charity toward your spouse—not because your spouse has done something you feel obligated to repay or because you will get anything in return but because your spouse is made to be loved, and you want to live your vow to love God and your spouse. Look at your spouse and hear Jesus speaking to you from within that person, asking, "Do you love me?" What is your response? Love Jesus in and through your spouse in ordinary ways with extraordinary love, with *agape* love.

Questions for Reflection

1. "Love is a gift, not a reward." Are you ever stingy with your love? If so, how can you be more generous with your spouse?

2. How can you develop and implement a routine to make sure your family prays together more often?

3. Are there any devotions that you and your husband or wife both gravitate toward (e.g., the Holy Rosary)? How can you use that devotion to anchor your prayers together?

4. "The couple needs to grow in love with God and with each other." When you draw closer to your spouse, do you also feel closer to God—and vice versa?

5. Imagine the Holy Family living together in Nazareth. What do you think their prayer routine was like? How can your family imitate theirs?

3

What God Has Joined

Immediately after the creation of Eve and the joyful exclamation of Adam, we read in the book of Genesis: "Therefore a man leaves his father and his mother and cleaves to his wife, and they become one flesh" (Gen. 2:24). Here is God's intention in creating humanity. The natural vocation of the human person is marriage. Of course, one may receive a specific call from God—the celibate priesthood or the consecrated life, for instance. But Christian marriage is also a vocation. So, although marriage may be the most natural state of life, the call to that life and the person with whom that life is to be shared need to come from God. Although it is the primordial state of life, we saw that Original Sin and our own personal sins have made it very difficult to live married life in a truly fulfilling manner without God's help. But, if it is difficult with the person God chose for you, how difficult it must be if you choose a person who was not the person God intended for you!

This means that people have to pray about their vocation. Because marriage is the most natural vocation, most people assume they are called to marriage. But if they have never prayed about their vocation, how will they be certain? Even having said that, many people have already determined what they want to do, so they are not interested in whether God has something else planned for them. When they pray, they tell God what they think He wants for them rather than asking Him what He wants.

If you are certain God is calling you to marriage, the next thing is to pray about the person God has chosen to be your spouse. Discernment is necessary both in prayer and in your relationships with potential spouses. It is imperative that you stay in the state of grace so your discernment remains clear. According to Catholic moral theology, it is impossible for a person in the state of mortal sin to think clearly. This does not mean you are unable to do your job or take a test if you are in the state of mortal sin. It means your ability to think clearly is inhibited in the area of the sin and in those areas ancillary to it.

For example, if two persons are sinning against one another in impure ways, their minds will be cloudy regarding purity and in the related areas such as growth in love and clarity of discernment concerning the person or the relationship. The purpose of the dating relationship is to discern whether the person one is dating is the right person to marry. It is also to grow in love with each other. The love cannot grow if the persons are sinning together, because sinning against each other is the opposite of loving each other. Their discernment will be clouded because elements are introduced into the dating relationship that are intended only for a man and a woman united in marriage. For persons who are dating, any intimacy that is reserved for marriage will cause the same kind of unity on an emotional level and will make it hard for them to know whether they are right for each other.

Of course, if you are already married, it is even more necessary for you to pray for your spouse. Because of your union, you will either build each other up or pull each other down. Prayer for the other person is the greatest work of charity, so prayer will automatically open your heart with greater charity for your spouse. Prayer is always necessary, but it takes on greater gravity when things are difficult in the relationship or when forgiveness is necessary. It is difficult to pray for someone you are angry with, but praying for that person will help to cut through the anger and bring peace and reconciliation to the relationship.

Since marriage is a vocation—that is, a call from God—married life should have God at its center. However, we know that marriage is a part of every culture, many of which have no reference to God. This helps us to understand the distinction the Church makes between two levels of marriage: natural marriage and sacramental marriage. A sacramental marriage exists when two baptized persons are united in marriage by God. People who are not baptized do not have the capability of entering into a sacramental marriage. The simple reason for this is that Baptism is necessary in order to receive any of the other sacraments. In the case of marriage, the philosophical principle that the greater subsumes the lesser holds true. This means that a sacramental marriage is also a natural marriage.

Because marriage is something God created from the beginning for the fulfillment of the couple as well as the foundation of society, a natural marriage is recognized as a valid marriage even when the unbaptized couple does not know God or practice a revealed religion. For a natural marriage to be valid, four conditions must be satisfied:

1. The marriage must be entered into by one man and one woman.
2. It is established by and between the two parties by consent.

3. It is entered into as an irrevocable, exclusive partnership for the whole of life.

4. It is entered into for the good of the spouses and for the procreation and education of offspring.

These requirements are stipulated in the *Code of Canon Law*, canon 1055.

These four elements comprise the natural law requirements for any marriage to be valid. As mentioned, natural marriage has no intentional relationship to God and to His revealed law, but the natural law is written into the heart of every person. These same elements that make up a natural marriage are also found from the beginning in the marital union of Adam and Eve. God provided guidance for Adam and Eve to live with Him and with each other by entering into a covenant with them.

Covenants establish a relationship between the parties involved. There are many examples of natural-level covenants, but the covenant we will consider is an agreement between God and His people in which God makes promises to the people and the people make promises to God. God has entered into numerous covenants over the centuries, several of which are public—for instance, those with Noah, Abraham, Moses, David, and Jesus. Obviously, the number of marital covenants since the inception of the Church is almost innumerable. Covenants have a sign to remind us of something both grave and glorious. The most familiar is the sign of the covenant God made with Noah: the rainbow, which symbolizes the promise God made never to destroy the whole world by a flood again (Gen. 9:13–17). Another aspect of most covenants is that they are sealed in blood. This sealing can be seen in Exodus 24:5–8, when Moses sprinkles the blood of oxen on the altar and on the people. Another part of a covenant people often forget about is the consequences that follow if the covenant is broken. The clearest example of this is found in Deuteronomy 27–30, which describes both the curses for disobedience and the blessings for obedience. It is interesting to look at what God told the people over 3,500 years ago and then apply it to what we see happening today.

In God's providence, marriage is established for the good of the spouses, of the children, and of society, but marriage builds upon the foundation that has already been laid down by God through faith, hope, and charity. As mentioned earlier, Adam and Eve entered into a covenant with God that established the pattern God intended for married life: the couple would be united in an agreement with God and with each other. As history moved forward from the Garden of Eden and God entered into covenants with Noah, Abraham, and Moses, some people were not included in the covenants while others chose to leave them. For those in a covenant relationship with God, their marriages were built upon the covenant already in place. These couples were held to a higher accountability because of the added elements of the covenant that augmented the elements of natural marriage. If they were faithful to the terms of the covenant, their marriages were objects of profound blessing by the Lord; if they were disobedient, there were profound consequences.

This discussion may appear interesting but irrelevant; in reality, however, it is essential to understand. God entered into a covenant with the Jewish people through Abraham. The sign of the covenant for the Jewish people is the mark of circumcision. This may seem a little gross to us, but it is a reminder of the covenant every time a couple engages in the conjugal embrace. The covenant for the Jewish people is something outside themselves — that is, an external agreement. In this covenant, the Jewish people are established as the People of God. Building upon the covenant with Abraham, God added the covenant He made with Moses. The Ten Commandments were the terms of this covenant. The covenant, then, was written in stone; again, an agreement that was external to the people.

Of course, external covenants are still binding. As mentioned, the covenant with Abraham made the Jewish people the People of God. It created a spiritual bond that united everyone who was incorporated into the covenant through the sign of circumcision. This covenant defined the people in their relationship with God. Because God is faithful to His covenants, He will always maintain what He has promised. This establishes the relationship between the married couple, who are incorporated into the covenant with each other and with God. What God stated in the Garden of Eden regarding the marriage between Adam and Eve is demonstrated more profoundly in the marriages of the people of the covenant, the Jewish people. They become one flesh. There is a true union, but just as the sign of the covenant is incised into the flesh, so the union built upon this covenant is a union of the flesh.

What's more, a covenant of marriage is to be sealed in blood. For the Jewish people, the covenant that makes them the People of God is sealed in the blood of the male in the ritual of circumcision. Also, for the Jewish people, the union that makes the two to be one flesh is sealed in the blood of the female. Sacramental marriage is also a covenant, so it, too, is sealed in the blood of the female. Notice in both the male and the female, the area where the covenant is sealed has to do with the union of the flesh and the giving of new life.

Still, we need to ask, why did God make two covenants with the people of Israel? The first was the covenant He made with Abraham, which made the Israelites the People of God. The second was with Moses, which brought the people of Israel into a marriage covenant with God. The covenant God made with the Israelites through Moses brought the people much closer to God because, in this second covenant, God became the Bridegroom of Israel. This marriage covenant was sealed in blood on the day Moses slaughtered oxen and sprinkled their blood on the altar and on the people (see Exod. 24:5-8). In other words, this marriage covenant was not only holy: it was an act of worship.

With this second covenant as its foundation, the marriage of a Jewish man and a Jewish woman was modeled after this liturgical act of the marriage covenant between God and His Chosen People. The Jewish people understood their marriages to be a covenant between the couple and God. This can be observed in several features of a Jewish wedding. First of all, in ancient Israel, the groom would dress as a priest. The marriage itself took place in a wedding chamber, which was made to resemble the tabernacle built in the desert by Moses. Also, there are no vows in a Jewish wedding. The groom puts the ring on the bride's finger and pronounces her to be his wife. This is what takes place in the wedding chamber. In other words, this is the liturgical ritual of the marriage; the contractual or covenantal aspects of the marriage were worked out and put in writing *before* the liturgical ceremony. This follows the pattern we see with God's giving the terms of the covenant in the Ten Commandments, written on stone tablets, and then formalizing the marriage in the liturgical ceremony.

This is beautiful, but God was not finished. The people of Israel were not always faithful to their covenant, both in general and within their marriages. Even with the covenant relationship, the damage caused by Original Sin was so extensive that the people were not able to remain faithful. Part of this, as St. Paul tells us, is that no one is justified by the law (Gal. 3:11). The covenant was intended to help the people become holy; without righteousness, however, the people would seek ways to evade the terms of the covenant rather than to obey them. Again, this is what happens with agreements that are external to us. We can easily see the terms of the covenant as a set of rules or ordinances that need to be followed. One is not going to become holy by just going through the motions, even the correct motions. For this reason, God promised a new covenant through the prophets. This promise is made most explicitly in Jeremiah 31. Here God states that the new covenant will not be like the old one; instead, the Lord says that He will write His law upon our hearts (Jer. 31:31–33).

The covenant God made with the people of Israel through Moses was written in stone; the New Covenant is written on human hearts (2 Cor. 3:3). However, it is also important to recognize the difference between this New Covenant and the covenant God made with Abraham, which was in the flesh. In the covenant with Abraham, the foreskin of the males was removed. The foreskin was flesh, but it was an external part of the body. In fact, it was external to an external part of the body. God tells us through Jeremiah that the New Covenant will be written upon our hearts. This is something internal and intrinsic and life-giving to the person. So we are beginning to see a fundamental change in the way God will relate to His people.

It is through the prophet Isaiah that God makes the most astounding revelation about this New Covenant. Four "Suffering Servant Songs" are included in Isaiah 42, 49, 50, and 52–53. These passages foretell the sufferings of the Messiah, and each passage refers to the Messiah as the "Servant" of the Lord. In each of the first two Suffering Servant Songs, one sentence is of interest to us. The first song says of the Messiah, "I have given you as a covenant to the people" (42:6). In the second song, we read: "I have kept you and given you as a covenant to the people" (49:8). Because we know who the Messiah is, we can address the point with reference specifically to Jesus. Notice in these verses that God is not making a covenant with His Servant; rather, the Servant *is* the covenant. So the New Covenant is a person: the Person of Jesus Christ!

Before we continue, we should mention a few conditions that may prevent a couple from forging a marital covenant—that is, from contracting a valid marriage. Some of these reasons involve situations in which a couple wants to marry but the Church will not allow the marriage. The Church must consider, for instance, whether the couple are old enough to marry; whether they both consent to the union; whether they are closely related by blood; or whether they are already married, either in or outside the Church.

There are also situations in which the couple has made marriage vows, but the Church does not accept them. This means that because something was seriously wrong at the moment the couple made their vows, some marriages are invalid. A marriage might be invalid because one or both of the spouses was unable to understand the nature and responsibilities of married life or to assume the obligations of marriage; because one spouse deceived the other into getting married; because one or both of the spouses failed to intend the good of the other; or because something was not correct in terms of the matter or the form of the sacrament or in terms of the intention regarding permanence, fidelity, or openness to life. In other words, something must be seriously wrong to declare a marriage invalid.

Let's look at this question of validity from the perspective of the Mass. If someone claimed that a Mass was invalid, we would need to ask why. "It just didn't feel right" would not be an acceptable reason for such a claim. If there was not bread and wine, if there was not a validly ordained priest, if the priest said the wrong words at the consecration, or if the priest stated that he did not intend to change the bread and wine into the Body and Blood of Christ, then there would be objective reason to say the Mass was invalid. Without such evidence, the Mass must be assumed to be valid. The same is true with Holy Matrimony. Unless there is objective evidence to support a claim that a marriage was not valid, the marriage must be assumed to be valid.

Because of the holiness of the sacraments, the Church is very protective of them and of the people involved. For this reason, if someone believes a marriage to be invalid, the Church will begin a formal process to investigate and evaluate the evidence for such a claim. This process is conducted to determine whether something was seriously wrong when the marriage vows were professed that would cause the marriage to be invalid. Remember, the sacrament takes place (or fails to take place) at the moment when the vows are exchanged. If someone is unfaithful at some point after the marriage, it violates the marriage vows, but it does not invalidate the sacrament. So the investigation regarding the validity of a marriage looks at the circumstances at and around the time of the marriage itself.

If the investigation determines that something was seriously wrong at the time of the marriage, a Declaration of Matrimonial Nullity (commonly referred to as an annulment) would be granted. This is an ecclesial decision that, even though a civil marriage did occur, a sacramental marriage did not occur. Therefore, if the couple was not sacramentally united, they are free to marry. If, on the other hand, the marriage is found to be sacramental, the two remain united in marriage until the death of one of the spouses.

Church law requires Catholics to be married according to Catholic form — in other words, in a church building, in front of a priest or a deacon, using the liturgy of the Church. Dispensation from Catholic form can be given for a Catholic to marry a non-Catholic in a Protestant church building. Without a dispensation, the Church will not recognize the marriage as valid. However, if two baptized Protestant persons are married, the Church will recognize their marriage as valid. Since neither person is a baptized Catholic, they are not bound by the laws of the Catholic Church, so they are not required to be married according to Catholic form. Also, if a baptized Catholic wants to marry a baptized Protestant who is divorced from his or her first spouse, the Catholic Church does not allow the marriage unless a Declaration of Matrimonial Nullity is granted to the Protestant spouse.

Before any investigation of a marriage can even be commenced, divorce proceedings in the civil courts must be completed and the final divorce decree must be issued. We will speak about the unity and indissolubility of marriage later, but for now, we will say that to divorce a spouse without very serious reason is a sin against the matrimonial vows and covenant. The Church recognizes that there are reasons a couple must separate — for example, in cases of physical or psychological abuse. Yet separation should be considered a last resort. The Church also recognizes that there are some situations in which a civil divorce may be the only means of ensuring certain legal rights, such as the care of children or the protection of inheritance. In such cases, civil divorce may be tolerated. The granting of a civil divorce, however, does not free the couple of their matrimonial obligations. As we have seen, the Church must uphold the sacramentality of the marriage until it is proven invalid. This means that the couple, even though they are apart, must still live according to the vows of their marriage. They may not enter into romantic relationships of any kind — though, of course, they are urged to rekindle their own marital love. This isn't always possible, but it is hoped for.

Our Lord teaches that if a man divorces his wife and marries another woman, he commits adultery against her; the same is true of a divorced woman who marries another man.

The Church wants to make sure the minds and hearts of the faithful are at peace and do not have to question whether a sacrament was validly conferred. For this reason, the Church requires that all sacraments consist of objective criteria that anyone of sound reason can judge. In each of the sacraments, three criteria must be present simultaneously for the sacrament to be valid: the *matter*, the *form*, and the *intention of the minister*.

Matter concerns the sensibly perceptible aspects of each sacrament. Just as the Eucharist, for example, requires bread and wine, so Matrimony requires a baptized male and a baptized female who are both free to consent to be married.

Form has to do with the words or the formula used in the confection of a particular sacrament. Again, using Mass as an example, "This is my Body" and "This is the chalice of my Blood" are the words that must be spoken by the priest. Any deviation from that formula, for any reason, would cause the Eucharist to be invalid. In Holy Matrimony, the form is the words of the vows. The Church allows the couple to choose from two sets of vows, both being equally valid. During the 1980s and 1990s, it was popular for couples to write their own vows. Those vows may have been meaningful to the couple at the time, but, unfortunately, many of those marriages were not valid sacramental marriages. Some couples like to memorize the vows, but the concern is they might state them wrong during the ceremony when they are under pressure. Remember, a sacrament is valid not because you want it to be, but because it was done correctly.

The intention of the minister of the sacrament is equally important because if one person does not have the intention to do what the Church intends in the sacrament, then the sacrament is invalid. For example, when a priest talks to the children preparing for First Holy Communion, he might bring an unconsecrated host to the classroom and ask the children at what point in the Mass the bread changes into Jesus. When the correct answer is given, the priest might say, "Right! When I say, 'This is my Body,' that is when the bread becomes Jesus." The priest has the right matter and the right form, but he has no intention of changing that piece of bread into Jesus in the classroom.

This point about the intention of the minister takes on even greater importance in the sacrament of Holy Matrimony because it is not the priest who is the minister of the sacrament. Rather, the bride and groom are the ministers of the sacrament to each other. The task of the priest (or deacon or bishop) is to be the witness of the Church to verify that the matter, the form, and the intention are present and correct.

This is why, immediately before the couple professes their vows in the Ordinary Form of the Rite of Matrimony, the priest will ask them three questions about their intention. In essence, because Matrimony is also a covenant, the intention must satisfy the three constituent elements of a marriage covenant. Both persons must intend the marriage to be permanent—that is, until one of them dies. Both persons must also intend to be faithful in the marriage. Finally, both persons must intend that the marriage be open to life—that is, both persons must be willing to accept children and not intentionally place anything in the way of conceiving a child. If any one of these intentions is not proper, then there is no sacrament, although the state may still recognize the union as a legal or civil marriage. It is precisely because the sacrament of Holy Matrimony is the union of two baptized persons who are the ministers of the sacrament to each other that the Catholic Church accepts the marriages of non-Catholic Christians as being valid sacramental marriages.

In the United States, the government allows religious ministers to serve as *legal* witnesses to the civil marriage. In most countries, a couple must go to a judge one day and go to the church on another day because the Church does not accept the state's marriage and the state does not accept the Church's marriage. Allowing the priest to be the witness for both the Church and the state means that a couple needs to plan only one ceremony. This is also the reason the couple must have a marriage license from the state before getting married in the Church. The exception to this is when a couple who is civilly married wants their marriage to be sacramental. This occurs when two people (at least one of them a baptized Catholic) have professed their vows before a judge or were married in a Protestant ceremony without a dispensation from the bishop. In such a marriage, the Catholic spouse would not be able to receive Holy Communion because, for a Catholic, entering a marriage that is not a sacrament is a mortal sin. In this situation, the couple would need to make their vows before a priest in a marriage ceremony known as convalidation.

The point of mortal sin brings up another question that is raised with some frequency: What if someone was in the state of mortal sin when he or she was married? (The same question applies to Confirmation and Holy Orders.) In this situation, assuming the matter, the form, and the intention were correct, the marriage would still be valid and would still be a sacrament. However, because one needs to be in the state of grace in order to receive grace, the grace of the sacrament would not be efficacious for the person in the state of mortal sin at the time the sacrament was confected. Once the person goes to Confession and is returned to the state of grace, all the graces that would have been given at the moment of marriage become efficacious retroactively.

In each of the sacraments, there is an increase in sanctifying grace, which is God's life in us. However, each sacrament provides graces specific to that particular sacrament. The sacramental graces that come with Holy Matrimony are many because God offers spouses the graces necessary for everything that will occur in the course of their married life. Of course, God will not force His grace on anyone, so the couple must open their hearts to receive these graces. In a general way, these graces include the grace to live with each other, to bear each other's faults, to help each other to grow in sanctity, to be good parents, to help with the difficulties that will inevitably arise, to fulfill the duties of Christian spouses and parents, and to live alone with each other after the children have been raised.

In addition to these sacramental graces, Fr. John Hardon, S.J., identifies four specific kinds of grace given in marriage and seven virtues that are given with these graces.[1] These graces include an increase in the indwelling of the Trinity for each spouse, an increase in sanctifying grace, the perpetual and exclusive bond of marriage, and the perfecting of the couple's love. The seven virtues Fr. Hardon enumerates are generosity, selflessness, humility, patience, joy, chastity, and loyalty. All of these are given at the moment of marriage, but in seminal form. The spouses need to work with God and with each other to make these virtues grow. God's grace makes these virtues attainable; however, grace does not make it easy to achieve these virtues. We must remember that virtues grow only when they are tested. The fullness of a virtue is not normally infused, but the grace necessary to attain a virtue is infused.

---

[1] Described in an article by Don Fier, "The Effects of the Sacrament of Matrimony," *Wanderer*, May 25, 2017.

These graces are available because marriage has been raised to the level of a sacrament. However, three essential properties of marriage—unity, indissolubility, and procreativity—are part of natural law, which God has written into our hearts. Because they are part of natural law, these properties apply to all marriages: natural and sacramental.

First, the *unity* of a marriage refers to the exclusivity of the relationship between one man and one woman; this flows from the equal dignity of the husband and wife. Because of the equal dignity of the spouses, the unity of the marriage is expressed in a particular way by the mutual and total love unique to married life. The second essential property of marriage, *indissolubility*, refers to the perpetual nature of the marital relationship due to the irrevocable personal consent of both spouses.

The properties of unity and indissolubility in marriage cannot be separated from each other. Both are commenced simultaneously at the moment the man and woman freely consent to the marriage vows. Indeed, marriage is indissoluble precisely because of the unity of the couple, even for a marriage on the natural level. The couple's vow is in no way contingent. Both freely consent to a union until death. Therefore, it is not possible for the state to dissolve a marriage, even though it may claim to do so by giving a decree of civil divorce. If marriage was only about providing goods and services, such a contract could be broken if the terms of the contract were not fulfilled. But even in a marriage contract for the state, the two spouses vow to be married for life. No escape clauses that allow a dissolution are built in.

In Christian marriage, which is also a covenant, the unity and indissolubility of marriage receive a deeper meaning because the marriage covenant between husband and wife is linked with the marriage covenant between God and His people. Therefore, the unity and indissolubility of marriage reflect the absolutely faithful love of God and His fidelity to the covenant.

With marriage being raised to a sacrament, the properties of unity and indissolubility receive an even deeper meaning and gravity. This is because the sacrament of Holy Matrimony builds upon our incorporation into Christ in Baptism, as we have seen, and also reflects the marital relationship between Jesus and His Church (see Eph 5:32). Just as the marriages of the Jewish people were modeled after the pattern of the marriage covenant between God and His people, now sacramental marriage is modeled after the pattern of the marriage of Christ the Bridegroom and His Bride, the Church. Christian marriage, then, must reflect and participate in the unity and indissolubility of the bond between Christ and the Church, brought about through our Lord's self-sacrificing love on the Cross. This sacrifice established a New Covenant into which the spouses are baptized and upon which the sacrament of Holy Matrimony is built.

In the mutual incorporation between God and the human person that occurs at Baptism, the person dwells in God and the Holy Trinity dwells in the soul of that person. Now, two persons in the state of grace who marry each other form a new communion of persons, and because both are in the Lord and the Lord is in both persons, they bring God into their union. In fact, God causes the new union on the spiritual level and forges a bond that is unbreakable by any worldly force. So in the sacrament of Holy Matrimony, grace augments the unity and indissolubility, raising them to a level that is not present in marriages that are merely natural. An act of divine power to unite the couple can be undone only by an act of divine power. This happens when God calls the soul of one of the spouses away from the union of the couple to the greater union of the saints.

God's Plan for Your Marriage

Having spoken about what it means to say that Holy Matrimony is a sacrament and how God unites the couple in this sacrament, we still need to ask the question of what is united. In each level of marriage, a real unity of the couple takes place, but in a sacramental marriage, grace brings a spiritual reality into this unity. What is united in this sacrament, and what are the implications of this union?

This question brings us back to our Lord's teaching, a teaching found nowhere else in Scripture: "What God has joined, let not man put asunder" (Matt. 19:6; Mark 10:9). In what may be the most important question among all the reflections in this book, we must ask: "What did God join?" Is it the bodies of the couple, as might be suggested by the passage our Lord quotes from the book of Genesis: "the two become one flesh"? It is true that in natural marriage and sacramental marriage, the two become one flesh. But is it God who joins the flesh of the married couple?

The body is the expression of the person. When we make an act of the will, that act is expressed physically in and through the body. This same logic must be applied to the marital union, but it can also be applied to situations in which two people have made an act of the will to engage in fornication, adultery, or any other such sinful act. St. Paul tells us that if a man engages in an act of intercourse with a prostitute, he becomes one body with her; St. Paul quotes Genesis 2:24 — "the two shall become one flesh" — to make his point clear (1 Cor. 6:16). The act itself is unitive.

In a sacramental marriage, the conjugal embrace is the physical expression of the spiritual union that takes place at the moment of the marriage. When the couple professes their vows, God works in a wonderful way to unite the couple in a spiritual union. It is this spiritual union of the two persons that is expressed in the physical union of the two. So it is true that the couple has made an act of the will, but God has also made an act of the divine will to cause the two to be united. This is why any sexual act outside of marriage is a lie; that is, the persons involved are trying to express something that does not exist.

Sexual intercourse has the effect of *consummating* a sacramental marriage. Once a valid union has been consummated, there is no dispensation from marriage vows that allows a married person to live as though he or she were not married. Given this truth, if there is no dispensation from a valid sacramental marriage, it is because there is something that makes the union of a sacramentally married couple literally indispensable. If a married person chooses to separate from his or her spouse or even to obtain a divorce in the civil courts, the Church recognizes the couple to be still married. Remember, no man can separate what God has united. Just as a priest who leaves active ministry is still a priest, so a married person who leaves his or her marriage is still married.

In a civil marriage, the state recognizes that the couple is united in marriage. If neither of the spouses is baptized, the Church will recognize the marriage as a valid natural marriage. However, it is merely a contractual union. In other words, what holds the couple together, from the perspective of the state, is a piece of paper saying they are married. The state allows them to break that contract and sign a new one with someone else. The state is not concerned with how many times you enter or break these contracts, as long as there is only one contractual agreement at a time (in most states). If a Catholic person attempts to enter this union without a dispensation from the bishop allowing the marriage, the Church will not recognize the marriage as valid. Without a dispensation, it is a civil marriage, with everything guaranteed by the state (legitimacy of birth, inheritance rights, and so forth), but there is no sacramental marriage, and therefore, the souls of the couple are not united by God.

God's Plan for Your Marriage

We know Holy Matrimony is also a covenant, so does God simply declare the couple to be united, or does He actually unite something? Is entrance into a sacramental marriage God's way of saying that because the vows were made to Him, it is now permissible for the couple to engage in relations and start a family? Is the only difference between natural marriage and sacramental marriage the grace a couple receives in the sacrament?

Holy Matrimony is a sacrament of the Church. Each of the sacraments does something to the soul. Three of the sacraments—Baptism, Confirmation, and Holy Orders—actually make an indelible mark on the soul. The sacrament of Penance removes sins from the soul. Anointing of the Sick removes sins and prepares the soul for eternal life. Most importantly, in the Holy Eucharist, there is a real union of the soul with Jesus. So, too, must Holy Matrimony cause something to *happen* in the soul.

The thesis here is that, at the moment a couple is married, the two souls are united in an accidental union (more on this below). The two actually become one. In other words, when Jesus said God has joined the couple, it means He really did join the two persons—not just juridically, but in a real and true union of the persons. At the beginning of their wedding, the couple enter the sanctuary as two; at the end of the ceremony, they leave the sanctuary as one. Pope St. John Paul II hinted at this when he said: "Conjugal love involves a totality, in which all the elements of the person enter.... It aims at a deeply personal unity, the unity that, beyond union in one flesh, leads to forming one heart and soul."[2]

When we talk about an accidental union, we are not talking about something that was a mistake. *Accidental* is used here in its

[2] Pope St. John Paul II, post-synodal apostolic exhortation *Familiaris Consortio* (November 22, 1981), no. 13, § 9.

philosophical sense to distinguish it from *substantial*. The three Persons of the Most Holy Trinity have a substantial union; the two natures of Jesus are united in a substantial union. This means they can never be separated. We know death ends the marriage, and therefore, there is a separation of the two when one of the spouses dies. The union in marriage cannot be substantial, but it is accidental.

Beyond that, if we get to Heaven, our souls will be united to God in an accidental union forever. Heaven is a marriage; Christian marriage is a prefiguration of eternity.

The term *accidental union* is used here merely to distinguish it from substantial union, but, in truth, the idea of an accidental union may be too vague and broad. There are many kinds of accidental unions that are far less than the union of a couple in Holy Matrimony. What it being said here, though, is that there is a real and true union of persons—of souls—that occurs when the couple professes their vows in a sacramental marriage. At that moment, God, who created the couple to be two separate persons, now re-creates them to be one.

Many married couples think it is sad that they will be separated at death. They wonder, when they are so much in love, why their souls cannot be united forever. They want to remain united to each other in Heaven. The truth is that marriage ends at death because something even greater—a union even more intimate—is awaiting them in Heaven. In other words, marriage does not end at death because there is something lacking. Rather, marriage ends so that the spouses can enter fully into the eternal marriage covenant foreshadowed and prefigured by the matrimonial covenant they share in.

In this heavenly marriage, we will all enter the fullness of what began the moment we were baptized and became members of the

Bride of the Lamb. In our union with the Lamb, there will be an intimacy far greater than the intimacy enjoyed in Christian marriage. Spouses will be united not only with each other but with every other soul in Heaven. To the fullness of our ability, we will know and love everyone perfectly, and we will be known and loved by everyone perfectly. Everyone together makes up the Mystical Body of Christ, which is also the Bride of Christ and the Church in glory, so we will be united with one another as the Bride, and we will all be united to Jesus, the Bridegroom of our souls. What God has joined in marriage on Earth will be perfected in the Communion of Saints in Heaven when the Bridegroom and the Bride will be united as one forever and when God will make all things new.

Questions for Reflection

1. Did you discern your marriage as a vocation through prayer? How did you know God was calling you to marry your spouse?

2. What does it mean for you that your marriage is a covenant? How might you be more faithful to its "terms"?

3. If you're a man, how do you reflect the heavenly Bridegroom (Jesus Christ)? If you're a woman, how do you reflect the heavenly Bride (Holy Mother Church)?

4. Pick one of the seven virtues strengthened by the graces of marriage: generosity, selflessness, humility, patience, joy, chastity, and loyalty. How do you practice that virtue in your marriage? How can you grow in that virtue?

5. Do you treat your spouse as if you two were united, both in flesh and in spirit? If so, how?

4

The New Creation

Prior to their sin, Adam and Eve could live married life as God intended because there was no selfishness in their relationship. They were able to love each other completely and selflessly. However, sin brought a variety of problems into the conjugal relationship of the first couple and that of every couple thereafter. If Jesus wants marriage lived according to God's intention, what did He change to allow for that to occur?

I think we can find the answer to this question in St. Paul's Second Letter to the Corinthians, where He tells us we have become a "new creation" in Christ (5:17). Notice that he does not say we have been restored in Christ but that we have become a "new creation." This means that Jesus has elevated us to a higher level of being than what Adam and Eve enjoyed in the Garden. In fact, we have already seen that when we are baptized, we are raised to a supernatural or divine level of acting and being. We have become partakers in the divine nature (2 Pet. 1:4)! Having been redeemed means we now have a redeemed manhood and a redeemed womanhood whereby the grace of God allows us to live married life in a supernatural way. Before we can consider what this looks like, we have to go back to the beginning of the new creation so we can learn who we have become as a new creation in Christ.

The first words in the Gospel of St. John are "In the beginning." These mirror the words at the beginning of the book of Genesis. St. John certainly wants us to think back to Genesis when we read these words, but he is not content to leave us there. Instead, what we find in St. John's Gospel is a deliberate attempt, among other things, to show us that God has made a new creation in Christ. In fact, in the first two verses of his Gospel, St. John makes clear that Jesus is the Word and that all things were made through Him and for Him. St. Paul echoes these words in Colossians 1:16.

To call Jesus "the Word" has profound theological implications. For example, in the context of Creation, this title corresponds to God speaking in the first chapter of Genesis: "God said, 'Let there be light'" (Gen. 1:3). When God said this, He spoke a Word through which the light came to be. This is also what we read in the Psalms: "He spoke, and it came to be" (Ps. 33:9). St. John goes on to speak of Jesus as "life." Jesus confirms this when He says that the Father has life in Himself and "has granted the Son also to have life in Himself" (John 5:26). But St. John then says this life was light and "the light shines in the darkness, and the darkness has not overcome it" (John 1:5). This corresponds to what we saw on the first day of Creation, when there was a separation of light and darkness. In our first chapter, we said this had to do with the angels' choice for or against God.

St. John then calls Jesus the "true light that enlightens every man," the true light that allows those who receive it to become children of God (John 1:9, 12). After all of this, the Evangelist tells us that the Word became flesh and dwelt among us (John 1:14). In the previous paragraph, we saw the reference to the first day of

Creation; now we see the reference to the sixth day of Creation, the day on which the first human persons were created. In Genesis, it is revealed that we are made in the image and likeness of God. In the new creation in Christ, it is revealed that we become children of God. Then, as it was in the garden where God walked with Adam and Eve, we now have God, in the Person of Jesus, dwelling among us and walking with us.

From what we have described in the previous paragraph, the new creation addresses only the first and the sixth days of the original creation. This is because the trouble in creation is due to what rational creatures, both angelic persons and human persons, have done by their own free choices. In other words, the other material creatures—the earth, sun, water, trees, animals, and so forth—did not sin. Nothing that was created between the second day and the first half of the sixth day needed to be redeemed. The angels could not be redeemed because their choice was forever, but the effects of their choice had to be countered. By bringing the light of Christ into the darkness, the truth as well as the proper ordering of creation is reestablished. Humanity did not fall on the day of their creation, so the correlation to the sixth day of creation implies not only the redemption of humanity, but the new creation of humanity as the children of God.

We can see from what St. John is telling us that the angels' choice of either light or darkness was not a choice merely between good and evil, but the choice for God, who is light, or against God. The choice for God would unite them to the light and bring them into the Kingdom of Light forever. The choice against God would remove the angels from the light and plunge them into darkness forever. So, light is a Person; more specifically for the choice made by the angels, the light is Jesus, and the light shines through His humanity. This is what Satan and the fallen angels could not accept.

The choice made by Adam and Eve brought darkness into their souls, which were created to be filled with the light of truth, love, and life. The choice made by Adam and Eve, as well as our own choices to sin or to act in virtue like the angels, is not merely a choice between good and evil; it is also a choice for or against God, who is light. This choice will be expressed in and through our words and actions, which are either good deeds or evil deeds. In creating us anew, God delivered us from the dominion of darkness and brought us into the kingdom of His beloved Son (Col. 1:13). Therefore, we are not children of darkness or of night, but children of light and of the day (1 Thess. 5:5). By linking the concepts of darkness and night with light and day, we are brought right back to the first day of Creation. It is two kingdoms, the Kingdom of God and the kingdom of Satan. St. John tells us that God is light; in Him there is no darkness (1 John 1:5). This suggests that Satan is darkness and in him there is no light. St. Paul states this same truth very poignantly in his Second Letter to the Corinthians when he asks: "What partnership have righteousness and iniquity? Or what fellowship has light with darkness? What accord has Christ with Belial?" (6:14–15). Jesus told us: "I am the Light of the world" (John 8:12; 9:5). He also instructed us to, "Walk while you have the light, lest the darkness overcome you.... While you have the light, believe in the light that you may become sons of light" (John 12:35–36). Thankfully, the Light came into the darkness and the darkness was not able to overcome it, so the events of the first day of Creation have been reversed. Both the Light and the darkness remain, but now the choice is ours. St. John tells us that people did not want the light because their deeds were evil (John 3:19). The choice is clear and there are only two possibilities: the light is truth, love, and life; the darkness is lies, selfishness, and death.

With the disaster of the first day of Creation reversed and renewed, all that was needed was to re-create humanity in such a way that we would be able to take our rightful place in the restored order of creation. This would not be a simple task. We saw that when God began His creation, there was only a formless void. The Holy Spirit hovered over the waters and brought order out of the chaos; the order is love. The new creation, however, did not begin with a formless void because human creatures, the subject of this new creation, already existed. However, a human person, who is made for love but is unable to love in the manner for which he was created, is still a void of sorts — certainly not formless but void: unable to love and be loved fully and unable to enter into the pure love of Heaven. Jesus brings the love of God into the world and is thereby the life and light of the world. Jesus brings the love of God into our souls and is thereby the life and light of our souls. The way this order was accomplished is what we have to consider next.

We saw above how Jesus reversed what occurred on the first day. We also mentioned that since humanity did not sin on the sixth day, the first day of their existence, what Jesus does on the sixth day is not a restoration of what was in creation; rather, it is a reversal of the effects of sin and a new creation that makes us children of God and partakers of the divine nature. What we saw in the Prologue of St. John's Gospel is expanded and expounded in the rest of his Gospel. This is why there are a number of references to the light and the darkness in addition to the way God prepared for the remaking of humanity. It is not until near the end of St. John's Gospel that we see this new creation taking place.

In the first verse of his Gospel, St. John places us on the first day of the "old" creation. At the end of his Gospel, he places us on the sixth day, the last day of creation. Remember that, for the Jewish people, a day begins and ends at sunset, not at midnight.

In other words, at the moment the sun set on what we would call Holy Thursday evening, Good Friday began. This means that, according to the Jewish demarcation of days, the Last Supper took place on Friday, not on Thursday.

This is important because it was on the sixth day, Friday, that Jesus went out to the Garden of Gethsemane. Satan entered into the garden, as he had done with our first parents. Unlike our first parents, Jesus did not succumb to the temptations of the vile creature. Instead, He showed us the pattern of what Adam should have done. In other words, Adam should have eaten the fruit of the Tree of Life and then encountered Satan. Satan would have appeared to be victorious over Adam, but then Adam would have risen up and been victorious. Instead, as we know, this did not happen, and Original Sin brought with it a host of negative effects.

In the new creation, God, in the Person of Jesus, is betrayed in a garden, the Garden of Gethsemane. After the trials, Jesus carries His Cross to another garden. Calvary itself was a rocky outcrop, but it was surrounded by a garden where Jesus was eventually buried. In this garden, we see all the elements from the time of the Fall. We have a man, a woman, and a tree in a garden. The Man is crowned with thorns and covered with sweat—the punishment meted out to the man when the first sin was committed. The woman is united with the man but suffers terribly as she labors to give birth to her spiritual children. The pain in childbirth was the punishment meted out to the woman at the time the first sin was committed. The woman labors to give life; the Man labors to sustain that life. Of course, death was a punishment for sin as well, so we find that also in this tragic scenario.

From the Cross, Jesus speaks to His Mother and calls her "Woman" (John 19:26). This expression sounds extremely disrespectful, but it is not. Mary's name is never mentioned in St. John's

Gospel, in order to call attention to this exchange. The reference to Mary as "woman" hearkens back to Genesis 3:15, when God told Satan there would be enmity between the serpent and the woman. The events on Calvary are the fulfillment of what was spoken by God in response to Original Sin. What we see on Calvary is that Jesus is taking on the punishment given to men, while Mary is taking on the punishment given to women. Recognizing this, St. Paul calls Jesus the last Adam—or, in some translations, the new Adam (1 Cor. 15:45). A new Adam without a new Eve would not be complete, so our Lady becomes the new Eve. This new Eve (Mary) was not created from the opened side of the Man, but the Bride of the Man was created from His opened side.

What's more, Adam was put into a deep sleep—a kind of death—and his bride was created from his opened side. Now Jesus, the new Adam, enters the sleep of death, and from His opened side, His Bride is created. The Church is the Bride, made up of the spiritual children of the woman (recall that Eve is the mother of all the living, so our Lady is the mother of all those alive in Christ); these children are washed in water, symbolized by the water flowing from our Lord's side, and are fed with the Eucharist, symbolized by the Blood flowing from His side.

There are layers of meaning in the Gospel accounts, and the new creation is just one of these layers. However, one final piece links the events of the Crucifixion with the events of creation. In the book of Genesis, we read: "Thus the heavens and the earth were finished, and all the host of them. And on the seventh day God finished His work which He had done" (2:1-2). In St. John's Gospel, we read: "Jesus, knowing all was now finished said (to fulfil the Scripture) 'I thirst.' ... When Jesus had received the vinegar, He said, 'It is finished'" (19:28, 30). This phrase, "It is finished," can be interpreted in a number of ways, but the use of the word "finished" in Genesis and St. John suggests very strongly that we have to understand this phrase in the sense of the new creation. (In the next chapter, we will see another way this phrase can be interpreted.)

As it was in the original creation, our Lord rested on the seventh day from all the work He had undertaken. He took the humanity He had now redeemed and prepared it for the new dignity with which it would be endowed in the new creation. On the first day of the week, Christ rose from the dead, revealing a glorified humanity. Obviously, prior to our own resurrection, our humanity is not glorified. But the humanity of Christ, risen from the dead, gives us a glimpse of the dignity that is ours as members of Christ, children of God, and partakers of the divine nature. The resurrection signifies the new creation of humanity.

On the sixth day, our sins were nailed to the Cross (see Col. 2:14); that is, everything that separated us from God was removed. We were redeemed and renewed in the image and likeness of God. On the first day of the new creation, humanity, with its sins removed, is given a share in the glory of God.

Jesus possessed a humanity that was raised to a divine level, but that needed to be communicated to us so we could participate in this new creation. St. John tells us that after Jesus had risen from the dead, He appeared to His Apostles and breathed on them (John 20:22). In this appearance, Jesus gave the Apostles the authority to forgive sins, but the action of breathing on the Apostles goes back to the second chapter of Genesis, when God breathes life into the nostrils of Adam (Gen. 2:7). The Apostles were obviously already alive, so the life breathed into them was not natural life but supernatural life.

This gift was the Holy Spirit. It is the Holy Spirit who raises us to a supernatural level of acting and of being. Recall that at the beginning of creation, the Spirit hovered over the waters and brought order out of the chaos. Sin brought, and continues to bring, chaos into God's creation. Through the Holy Spirit, the forgiveness of sin and the infusion of grace and love into the soul of the forgiven sinner bring life, love, and order into the soul, which was mired in the chaos of sin and devoid of God's love. The soul that was like the void at the beginning of the new creation has now been so transformed that St. Paul can pray that we would be "filled with all the fulness of God" (Eph. 3:19).

This gift of the Holy Spirit and the re-creation of humanity took place on the eighth day, which is also the first day of the week. It was on the original first day that the fallen angels chose darkness over light. In the Resurrection and the breathing forth of the Holy Spirit, the darkness in which humanity dwelt because of sin was changed into light through the forgiveness of sins. This transformation is a radical transformation. The word *radical* means "at the root." Every human person is made in the image and likeness of God, but even with this dignity, humanity was still in the dark because of Original Sin. It is only in Christ that our dignity is transformed. The change is so radical that St. Paul can say of us: "You were darkness, but now you are light in the Lord" (Eph. 5:8). Notice he does not say we were *in* the darkness but we *were* darkness. Now we are not just *in* the light: we *are* light. This transformation affects us at the very depth of our being, which is why the transformation is radical.

To be light, or "sons and daughters of Light" (see John 12:36), implies living as children of God, free from sin and abiding in truth, love, and life. In essence, we have been living in that eighth day—the first day of the new creation—for more than two thousand years. The struggle between light and darkness continues in the soul of every person on Earth.

God began human creation with marriage, so it makes sense that the new creation should also begin with marriage. As we saw with Adam and Eve, they reached out in disobedience to grasp the forbidden fruit, and darkness came into each of their souls and into their relationship. With the grace won for us by Jesus on the Cross, married couples are able to live the way God intended from the beginning. Unfortunately, all of us are still bogged down by the effects of sin and have to fight hard to keep our souls filled with light.

The effects of Original Sin—death, sin, concupiscence (the inordinate desires of the flesh), the darkening of the mind, and the weakening of the will—remain in every human person. All of these, with the exception of death, can be mitigated to some degree through prayer, study, and growth in virtue, but they cannot be removed entirely. In other words, even in the new creation, we will not have the original integrity enjoyed by Adam and Eve before the Fall. Jesus has conquered death in His Resurrection, but like Jesus, each of us has to enter into death before we can share in the glory of the resurrection.

Three punishments also befell humanity because of Original Sin. Once again, two of them cannot be removed entirely. The pain in childbirth and the labor necessary to sustain life can be mitigated through modern medicine and technology, but there will always be pain with childbirth, and people will always need to work for a living. (It is part of our dignity to work as God worked in creation. Adam was to till the soil before the Fall, but the work became toil after the Fall.) These effects of Original Sin cannot be completely removed, but God has given us a means to reverse the punishments that affect our human relationships. The relationship between Adam and Eve, which was turned upside down by their punishment—that is, the man lording it over the woman while the woman's desire would be for the man—can be restored to the way it was supposed to be. By living married life according to God's will, the marital relationship will be correctly aligned. In other words, by exercising the redeemed manhood and redeemed womanhood of the new creation, married couples will gain a properly ordered relationship.

The means for attaining this properly ordered relationship is laid out for us very clearly in one of the most misunderstood passages in all of Scripture. In his Letter to the Ephesians, St. Paul tells women to be subject to their husbands, and he tells husbands to love their wives. This passage is one of the most beautiful in all of Scripture, but being so tragically misunderstood, the entire passage is not even read in some parishes. For this reason, we need to look more closely at what St. Paul says in order to determine how this passage provides for us the antidote to the punishment due to Original Sin that undermines the marital relationship. He writes:

> Be subject to one another out of reverence for Christ.
>
> Wives, be subject to your husbands, as to the Lord. For the husband is the head of the wife as Christ is the head of the church, his body, and is himself its Savior. As the church is subject to Christ, so let wives also be subject in everything to their husbands.
>
> Husbands, love your wives, as Christ loved the church and gave himself up for her, that he might sanctify her, having cleansed her by the washing of water with the word, that he might present the church to himself in splendor, without spot or wrinkle or any such thing, that she might be holy and without blemish. Even so husbands should love their wives as their own bodies. He who loves his wife loves himself. For no man ever hates his own flesh, but nourishes and cherishes it, as Christ does the church, because we are members of his body.

"For this reason a man shall leave his father and mother and be joined to his wife, and the two shall become one flesh." This is a great mystery, and I mean in reference to Christ and the church; however, let each one of you love his wife as himself, and let the wife see that she respects her husband. (5:21–33)

The first thing we need to address is the dreadful misunderstanding of a woman's being subject to her husband. Many people interpret this to mean that a woman is essentially a slave who is to jump at her husband's every command. This would be a violation of a woman's dignity. God created women in His own image and likeness and gave women a dignity that is absolutely equal to the dignity He gave to men. God also inspired the Sacred Scriptures, so to suggest that God would inspire St. Paul to write something that would not only violate the dignity of women but would also be contrary to God's own intention in both creation and in marriage is impossible.

With this point before us, we begin with the radical equality of the couple exactly the way St. Paul begins this important teaching. When reading this passage from Ephesians 5, many people skip or overlook the passage "Be subject to one another" and immediately begin at "Wives, be subject to your husbands." Taken in its fullness, St. Paul clearly is not asking anything of one spouse that he is not asking of the other. It is also clear that St. Paul is not demeaning women when he requires both husbands and wives to be subject to one another.

We need to consider first what to be "subject" means, since this word is central to the passage and is mentioned three times. The specific instruction of St. Paul is translated in different versions of Scripture with three words: *subject*, *submissive*, and *subordinate*. The Greek word used by St. Paul is from *hypotasso*, a word that is translated eight ways in the Revised Standard Version of the Bible. The word literally means "to place under," which is the meaning of *subject*. *Submissive* means "to be sent under," and *subordinate* means "to be under the order of." In our passage, the word is used in a passive form, so the more literal translation would be "being subject to one another." In other words, it is a free choice to place oneself under the other. This recalls St. Paul's advice to the Philippians to "do nothing from selfishness or conceit, but in humility count others better than yourselves" (Phil. 2:3).

It is also important to recognize that being subject to one another is not the same as being obedient to one another. While one who chooses to place himself or herself under another will choose out of love to be obedient to the other when asked, the concepts are two different realities connoted by two entirely different Greek words in Scripture. Having said this, it would not be inappropriate to mention the importance of obedience in the marital relationship. Recall that Original Sin was a matter of disobedience and that our salvation and redemption came about through the obedience of Jesus. The only thing we know about the "hidden life" of Jesus—that is, His life between the ages of twelve and thirty—is that He was obedient to Mary and Joseph (Luke 2:51). So important is this virtue that consecrated religious (monks, nuns, and so forth) make a vow of obedience.

Two lessons can be learned from the vow of obedience and its application in marriage for those who choose to be obedient by being subject to their spouse. First, any request must be made in charity—that is, for the good of the other. Second, the one making the request has the greater responsibility. The spouse choosing obedience is responsible for whether she is obedient; the spouse making the request will be responsible for the motive behind the request. The motive must be one of charity. We should also note that when one knows that the other is asking something out of pure love, it makes it much easier to accept and comply.

The point of being subject out of reverence for Christ is also of utmost importance for four reasons:

1. It reminds us that the couple is married *in* Christ. This union, because it is sacramental, is not only natural: it is supernatural. The union was created by God, and the presence of the Lord remains integral to the union of the couple.

2. We need to remember that we will all stand before the judgment seat of Christ one day. For those who are married, a major part of judgment will focus on their marriage and how the spouses lived the vows they made to one another and to the Lord.

3. Being subject to another is the Christian way. We are to do everything in and for the Lord. This sanctifies even our most natural and mundane tasks.

4. The word used by St. Paul in Ephesians 5:21, "Be subject to one another out of reverence for Christ," that is translated "reverence," is actually *fear*. Here, St. Paul is speaking of filial fear, not servile fear, hence the translation of "reverence." Servile fear is quaking in fear or being afraid of God. Once again, this is not the nature of Christian fear because we call God our Father and thus should not be afraid of Him. Filial fear is the fear of offending God because we love Him so much that we would never want to offend Him. This is not the fear of punishment that would come to us if we offend Him but the fear of doing anything that would grieve the Lord. Understood this way, being subject to one another is actually an act of love.

This filial fear of the Lord should also be the disposition of married couples toward each other. As St. Paul said, the subjection he requests of those who are married is for the Lord. This is a Christian approach to life. St. Paul instructs the Colossians: "Whatever you do, in word or deed, do everything in the name of the Lord Jesus, giving thanks to God the Father through Him" (Col. 3:17). Using the same line of thinking, it may be helpful to note that verse 21 of our current passage—"be subject to one another out of reverence for Christ"—is really the end of a much longer sentence that begins in verse 18. Verse 20 reads: "always and for everything giving thanks in the name of our Lord Jesus Christ to God the Father." This is the fundamental disposition Christian spouses should have toward each other. If everything is done for the Lord and with thanksgiving, married life would be as rich and beautiful as God has intended it to be.

After all, it's God who called you to this vocation, and it is to Him and to your spouse that you have made a vow to love your spouse. If you love your spouse in the Lord, you are loving the Lord *in* your spouse. St. Paul talks about how someone who is single can focus on pleasing the Lord and growing in holiness whereas a married person is divided because he or she has to focus on worldly affairs and how to please his or her spouse (1 Cor. 7:33–34). However, there is no division if the married person is striving to do the will of God. Since it is God who calls married people to marriage, striving to please one's spouse and fulfill the duties of the married state is pleasing to the Lord. A division exists in the person only when the person is not loving the Lord in his or her spouse and loving that spouse in the Lord.

Before we consider the particular implications of this passage, another aspect of this reading must be made clear. St. Paul speaks to wives and instructs them about how they are to live in the marriage relationship. These verses are for women. They are not for men to focus on and use against their wives. St. Paul goes on to instruct husbands about how they are to live in the marriage relationship. These verses are for men. They are not for women to focus on and use against their husbands.

In the quotation of the passage from Ephesians 5 given above, the word *subject* is used twice in two verses: "Be subject to one another out of reverence for Christ. Wives, be subject to your husbands, as to the Lord" (vv. 21-22). In the original Greek, however, the word is used only once, so a more literal translation from the Greek would be: "Being subject to one another in the fear of Christ; the wives to their own husbands as to the Lord." In other words, this instruction given to wives is a continuation of the previous directive: praying, being thankful to God in everything, and being subject to one another. So wives are to allow themselves to be subject to their husbands as a matter of love (filial fear) for the Lord. To love one's spouse in this manner is to love the Lord.

This is not a violation of a woman's dignity but is, rather, the very means by which a woman will find her dignity. Remember, St. Paul is addressing the aspect of Original Sin that adversely affects a woman in the marital relationship, that her desire would be for her husband. Being part of the punishment that came from Original Sin, this desire for one's husband is not what God intended for women from the beginning. The disorder is that the woman tries to exercise headship in the relationship. This might not sound too bad until one realizes the cost: in order to be the head, the woman has to relinquish being the heart in the relationship.

How are we to understand being subject, submissive, or subordinate in this context? It can be understood only by looking at the command St. Paul gives to husbands: to love their wives as Christ loved the Church (Eph. 5:25). This does not mean to have gushy feelings for your wife. It means to serve her. Indeed, the word St. Paul uses to instruct men regarding their love for their wives is *agape*, which, as we've seen, is the selfless kind of love that seeks only the good of the other. It is the kind of love with which God loves us. So, if a woman is to be placed under, be sent under, or be under the order of her husband, this means that she must be under the command given to her husband.

Yet the command to the husband is to love his wife. Therefore, being under this command, a woman must allow herself to be loved. She has to allow her husband's desire to be for her. If her husband is sent or ordered to love his wife, then being under this order reverses the part of Original Sin that most directly affects a woman in the marital relationship. For a woman to have her desire to be toward her husband is contrary to the receptive nature of a woman. A woman is being receptive, however, when she allows herself to be loved.

We see this receptivity in St. Paul's directive that wives should be subject to their husbands as the Church is to Christ. The Church receives her being from Christ, just as the first woman received her being from the first man. The Church receives from Jesus the fullness of truth, charity, and grace (the life of God). Therefore, a woman should receive from her husband true and life-giving love. The Church has been given a mission by the Lord to bring the truth, love, and life of God into the world. Therefore, a Christian wife receives from her husband the true and life-giving love and then gives this love to her husband, her children, and everyone she meets.

Husbands are commanded, as we have seen, to love their wives. Once again, this command is to set right the aspect of Original Sin that most directly affects men in the marital relationship: that a husband will lord his authority over his wife. To love means to do always what is best for the other. It means putting the other first and oneself last. To love is to serve. Moreover, if a woman's desire toward her husband is disordered because of Original Sin, we can deduce that the proper order is that a man's desire should be for his wife. To understand what this desire is, we have to recall what we saw in the first chapter, when we spoke of the creation of the woman and the joy the man experienced in the creation of someone who could receive his love and love him in return. In other words, the man is to initiate the love and give that love to his wife.

We have to be clear that when we speak of this desire for one's wife and the initiating of love, we are not referring merely to the sexual arena. While this is part of a husband's relationship to his wife, the sexual aspect is the microcosm of the whole relationship. In other words, the desire and initiation must be present in the whole of the relationship in order to be expressed in the intimacy of the couple. What does this mean? We have already spoken of this, but it means the man is to desire only the best for his wife and should actively provide for that. The man is to protect his wife so she can express the beauty of the feminine and open her heart to receive love so she can give love. Initiating love means recognizing the needs of one's wife and making strides to fulfill those needs. This implies that the husband should not have to be asked to meet the needs of his wife but should work constantly to anticipate those needs. A man's wife should be the beloved of his heart, and he should treat her as such.

In calling men to love and calling women to be subject to that love, St. Paul is directly addressing the weaknesses experienced by males and females in the conjugal relationship. Women generally do not have problems loving their husbands. Being relational, they perceive the needs of others, and they give and serve. However, women struggle to allow themselves to be loved by their husbands.

Men, on the other hand, have little trouble allowing themselves to be loved by their wives. Men will gladly soak up every ounce of love their wives are willing to give them. However, men struggle to love their wives. So, in telling couples to be subject to one another, St. Paul is essentially telling husbands and wives to keep doing what they do well, but work on the areas in which they do not do well.

Of course, St. Paul does not stop there. He also specifies what this looks like and gives us insight into the immense dignity of a sacramental marriage.

First, St. Paul tells us that as Christ is the Head of the Church, the husband is the head of his wife. Wives are instructed to be subject to their husbands the way the Church is subject to Christ. Once again, this does not sound very good to modern sensibilities. However, the next thing St. Paul says is that husbands are to love their wives as Christ loved the Church. Christ gave Himself up for her that He might present the Church to Himself in splendor, without spot or wrinkle, that she might be holy and without blemish (see Eph. 5:25–27). In other words, husbands are to sacrifice themselves for their wives in order to make their wives saints.

The husband's headship does not mean that he is better than his wife. Rather, it is taking account of the natural strengths of the male and the female as the two, being united in marriage, bring the fullness of humanity into their union. Obviously, both men and women have an intellect and a will, but men tend to operate more from the head whereas women tend to operate more from the heart. If the two are to be subject to one another, then it is, in this case, to receive strength from the other, learn from the other, and trust the other.

Having strengths of head and heart are certainly true of males and females respectively, but St. Paul is leading us to something deeper. Once again, he is addressing the manner by which a married couple reverses the catastrophe of Original Sin by living as men and women redeemed by Jesus Christ. Recall when Jesus told His apostles that they were not to lord their authority over one another. That's what pagan rulers do (Matt. 20:25–28). A husband is not the ruler of his wife, and so for a man to lord anything over his wife is not Christian. The task of the husband, like the task given to the apostles by Jesus, is to *serve* his wife.

This service will be given in many ways, but one area that needs to be addressed is that, as the head, the husband is to be the spiritual leader in the family. It is the husband's role to initiate prayer between the couple and, when there are children, with the whole family. Many studies have demonstrated the importance of the role of the father in the spiritual lives of the children. If the father goes to Mass, the children will be more likely to continue going to Mass when they are older. If the father does not go to Mass, even if the mother brings the children to Mass, the children will more often stop going to Mass as they get older.

And this is not limited to Mass attendance. A Christian marriage and a Christian family require daily prayer. This spiritual leadership is most effective when the husband takes seriously his role as the spiritual head of the family.

As we have seen, the fullness of humanity is present in the union of Matrimony. Each of the spouses is endowed with a head for truth and a heart for love, so, in a marriage, the spouses should be of one mind and one heart and sharing one life. This can happen only when both desire the truth and both are committed to love each other. As the couple learns to work together, this process will conform them to each other and the oneness of their marriage will grow in perfection.

In the human person, the intellect presents to the will certain perceived goods; the task of the will is to choose the highest good.

This is part of the service husbands and wives need to provide for each other. When decisions need to be made, husbands should look outward, in an objective or "big picture" way, and present possibilities to their wives. Women look at things in a more relational and familial way, so they receive what is presented by their husbands and provide feedback. This can go back and forth until a mutual choice is made. As the head, the husband is to make the final decision, but only after receiving the input of his wife and determining what will be best for his wife and family. This process helps to break the selfishness that profoundly affects men, by requiring them to sacrifice their own wants and desires for a greater good.

What if the husband chooses the opposite of what the wife thinks is best? The wife does not have to agree with her husband's decision, but this is part of the subjection a woman can choose out of reverence for Christ. If the husband's decision is immoral, the wife must reject it and do what is right. Assuming the morality of the decision, if a woman knows she has been heard and trusts that her husband is choosing what he thinks is truly best for her and the family — even if she does not agree with the decision — she may be at peace. If, on the other hand, the decision is made selfishly, the wife will need to die to herself and support her husband, praying for him so that he may overcome his selfishness. Perhaps the most difficult task for the wife is to love her husband even when she knows that in a particular decision, he is not acting out of love for her. For both, this is where the reference to Christ is so important. Doing something for the Lord will automatically bring them to do what is best for the other, and they will love each other with the love they receive from the Lord.

The love a husband must have for his wife, according to St. Paul, is *agape* love. We have spoken of *agape* love as being the kind of love with which God loves us, but if we don't fully understand what that means, St. Paul provides a beautiful description. He tells husbands they are to love their wives as Christ loved the Church: He gave Himself up for her (Eph. 5:25). St. Paul speaks of cleansing the Church to make her splendid, without spot or wrinkle, and to be holy and without blemish (Eph 5:26–27). Jesus went to the Cross and died so the Church could be born from His side. The water flowing from His Sacred Heart represents the purification of the members of the Church through Baptism and Confession. The Church herself is perfect in truth and love, but the Church comprises human persons who are often far from perfect. This life is about overcoming our imperfections and growing in holiness. Everyone in Heaven is free from sin and without imperfections. Therefore, only when the last person enters Heaven will the Church have the absolute perfection of being without spot, wrinkle, or blemish.

Understood this way, a husband is to die to himself, to his selfish wants and desires, and to live for the perfection of his wife. Since St. Paul is asking the same from both persons, a wife must live for the perfection of her husband. Both are to help each other by pointing out, in charity, the faults they see and by guiding the other to grow in virtue. Both, as members of the Bride of Christ, the Church, are to strive to be holy and without blemish and to help the other to be so. This can happen only through prayer, frequent reception of the sacraments, and mutual charity. In this way, both spouses help each other to remove all their spiritual spots, wrinkles, and blemishes. The more we overcome our sins and grow in virtue, the more we are able to love.

We saw above that the water that came forth from the Sacred Heart of Jesus represents Baptism and the purification of the members of the Church. We can apply this idea of purification to the way a couple can help each other grow in holiness. St. John tells us that not only water but also blood came forth from our Lord's pierced Heart (John 19:34). This blood represents the Holy Eucharist and can be applied to the next sentences St. Paul writes to the Ephesians: "Husbands should love their wives as their own bodies. He who loves his wife loves himself. For no man ever hates his own flesh, but nourishes and cherishes it, as Christ does the church.... 'The two shall become one flesh'" (Eph. 5:28-29, 31).

However, in addressing this to husbands, St. Paul is, once again, focusing on an issue that is part of Original Sin. Men, by nature, are visual and physical. Women's bodies are obviously attractive to men. If a husband is lusting after his wife, being selfish, or using her body in any wrongful manner, he is failing to love her and therefore himself. This is also why it is so important for women to be modest. A woman's dignity must be upheld by her and by the men who interact with her, particularly her husband. Women are more prone to use their bodies to attract men, but the attention they receive in doing this is the wrong kind of attention. Such behavior indicates a failure of the woman to love herself and the other. Even within marriage, husbands have to be very careful to ensure they look at and treat their wives with dignity, respect, and charity, and wives must be careful to carry themselves in a dignified, respectful manner.

St. Paul tells us a man nourishes and cherishes his body as Christ does the Church. Jesus does this especially through the Eucharist. Because the Eucharist is the entire Person of Jesus Christ, the eucharistic Lord continues to sacrifice Himself for the members of His Body. He feeds His members by giving Himself entirely to them. In calling husbands to this kind of love, St. Paul is really calling them to do what they have vowed to do in their marriage.

They cannot give themselves as food to their wives, as Jesus can in the Eucharist, but they can "nourish" their wives spiritually through prayer and self-sacrificing charity.

Once again, the point must be made that St. Paul is asking the same of both husbands and wives. It is also interesting to note that these specific instructions given to the men correspond with the twofold nature of the service of a husband in marriage: to protect and to provide. The husband is to protect his wife's dignity and to provide for her needs, especially her spiritual needs. This is what it means that the man is the head, and it is this to which a woman is to be subject. Nothing here is demeaning to a woman. Rather, when a woman is loved as she should be by her husband, and she is able to receive that love, she can come to know truly her own dignity and live according to that dignity.

As we have seen, St. Paul's instructions are meant to reverse the effects of Original Sin in the man and woman and in the conjugal relationship. However, we also have to recognize that the effects of sin move us away from who we are created to be. We are created in the image and likeness of God. Although the image always remains, the likeness can be diminished. These are the spots, wrinkles, and blemishes that St. Paul mentions in Ephesians 5:21–33. If these effects are reversed, then we become more and more the persons we are created to be. We become more like God. More than that, when a couple is married and become one, their union resembles the union of Christ and the Church and also the union of the three Persons of the Trinity. This is how we are created to live. In the new creation, this is also our call to live godly lives as the Lord intended from the beginning when He made us in His image and likeness.

We have spoken about the relationship between Christ and the Church and how that relates to a husband and wife. Now we need to consider marriage in the new creation according to its relationship to God: to the Most Holy Trinity and to Jesus, who is God and man.

In the Holy Trinity, there are three Persons who are one. In marriage, there are two persons who are one. The union of the couple is not perfect, but it does reflect the Trinity. And as we saw earlier, the married couple cannot unite themselves; this union requires the creative work of God. Therefore, there are really three who are part of this unity: a man, a woman, and God. The husband, wife, and God are united in love, and, therefore, marriage in the new creation not only *reflects* the Trinity but, to some degree, *participates* in the love of the Trinity.

A married couple, having a likeness to God in their individual persons and in their union together, is called to participate in this likeness to the Trinity by knowing and loving each other. Just as the Persons of the Trinity give themselves as a gift to the other Persons and receive the other Persons as a gift, so in marriage there is a complete and total giving and receiving of persons. This giving and receiving is expressed most completely in the marital embrace of the couple. Making themselves completely vulnerable to each other, each person knows the other and the other's love in a new and profound way. This is what Scripture means when it reveals that Adam knew his wife (Gen. 4:1) and that Mary said to the angel, "I know not man" (Luke 1:34). In this same act, a married couple love each other, and their intimate union is the expression of that love. St. Thomas Aquinas tells us that as human persons, we cannot love what we do not know. This intimate union in marriage is truly extraordinary because the act of knowing and the act of loving are simultaneous, as in the Trinity. In this act of knowing and loving, a new person may come into existence.

So in the Trinity there are three Persons united in truth, love, and life. In the Incarnation, the two natures of Jesus, human and divine, are perfectly united in truth, love, and life. And in the new creation, a married couple committed to the Faith are united in truth and love; they also share one life, they participate in the life of grace, and they become the source of new life.

Prior to sinning, the first couple was given a command to be fruitful and multiply, to fill the earth and subdue it (Gen. 1:28). This is the first commandment ever given to humanity. Just as we can say that the First Commandment is the greatest or most important of the Ten Commandments, so we can say this first commandment to humanity is the greatest or most important. This command is also an invitation of the greatest dignity because it is an invitation to share with God in the work of creation. The animals were given a similar command, but it is fundamentally different as it is realized in animals. Animals operate merely by instinct and according to their nature for the propagation of their species. Human persons also propagate their species, but they use their intellect and will to choose freely to be fruitful and multiply. This means human persons bring knowledge and love and freedom into the equation.

We know that Adam and Eve used their intellect and free will to reach out to the Tree of the Knowledge of Good and Evil, to choose the forbidden fruit. They chose death over life. Moses gave the people of Israel the choice between life and death and pleaded with them to choose life. To this day, this same choice remains: if we act according to our dignity—that is, if we act according to truth and love—we choose life. If we act in opposition to our dignity, we choose death.

This choice makes perfect sense, but we can go even deeper to see our dignity more profoundly. A correlation exists among truth, love, and life. The more we are conformed to the truth, the more we will love; the more we love, the more we will share in the life of God. The more we share in the life of God, the more we will become like Him. The more we become like God, the more we will be conformed to truth and the more we will love. Everything God does, He does out of love, and so everything we do should be done out of love too.

Before they sinned, Adam and Eve simply loved; they received everything as a gift of love from God and from each other, and they responded by loving God and each other; that is, they gave themselves to God and to each other as a gift of love. There was no shame because there was no selfishness. Sin, on the other hand, is selfish; it also brings chaos into the order created by love. God's love is creative. We receive love from God; therefore, our love must be creative. For a married couple to choose not to be open to life is to choose not to love. Such a choice violates one's own dignity and the dignity of one's spouse and rejects the invitation of God to participate in the love, the beauty, and the joy of creation. We are created for love. When we choose not to love, we choose death. We reach out to the forbidden fruit and listen to the devil's lie, thinking God does not want what is best for us. In doing this, we choose to live the lie in selfishness rather than live the truth in love; we choose sin and death over charity and life.

Love, as we saw in chapter 1, overflows any kind of boundary we may try to put on it. Because God is infinite, He has no boundaries; but still, we can say that human persons, made in the image and likeness of God, and even more as children of God, are the overflow of the love of the three Persons of the Trinity for one another. The love of the Trinity becomes life-giving for us. At the same time, because God has chosen to grant married couples the dignity of participating in the work of creation, human persons are also the overflow of the love of the married couple. Every human person, therefore, is the living, tangible, enfleshed sign of the love of the parents, who provided the physical material for the child's creation, and of God, who provided the child's soul. For this reason, when God looks at us, He should see His love mirrored back to Him in a human form. At the same time, when parents look at their children, they should see the love they have for each other being mirrored back to them. The beautiful face of a child is the living expression of the love of the married couple.

We see, once again, the great dignity of the vocation to the married state. God loves us so much that He chose to create us in His own image and likeness. The human person is the pinnacle of God's material creation. Every human person is made for truth, love, and life. Therefore, every new life should be conceived in truth and love. This can take place only in the union of a married couple because, according to God's design, marriage is the only proper place for the conception and raising of new persons made in His image and likeness and made His children in Baptism. Married life, then, is not only a participation in God's work of creation; it is also a participation in the new creation. Indeed, as He did in the beginning of creation, God has made married couples the foundation of the new creation.

Questions for Reflection

1. "If you love your spouse in the Lord, you are loving the Lord in your spouse." How is God calling you to love Him through your husband or wife?
2. How are you, as a husband, called to be the head of your family? How are you, as a wife, called to be its heart?

3. What does it mean to be "submissive" to your spouse? How might you live out that virtue in your marriage?

4. As a husband, do you do enough to facilitate prayer in your family? As a wife, are you supportive and encouraging of your husband's spiritual leadership?

5

Consummatum Est

Jesus Christ, the Church's Bridegroom, speaks of marriage in a number of parables in the Gospels. Perhaps the most powerful one tells us that the Kingdom of Heaven is like a king who gave a wedding feast for his son (Matt. 22:1-9). The first miracle of our Lord and the beginning of His public ministry took place at a marriage banquet (see John 2:1-11). According to St. John, Heaven will be a marriage banquet (see Rev. 19:7-9). When we think of a marriage banquet, we may be tempted to think only of the reception. But we have to remember that for the Jewish people of Jesus' time, a marriage banquet lasted for seven days, and the actual marriage took place within the context of the banquet. They were not two separate events, as they are today. So when we hear that Heaven is a marriage banquet, we are to think not of dinner and dancing (St. Paul says Heaven "does not mean food and drink") but of the union of the Bridegroom and Bride.

The particular aspect of this union I want to address in this chapter is the consummation of the union. The final words our Lord spoke from the Cross — "*Consummatum est*," meaning "It is consummated" or "It is finished"—must be understood in the context of Jesus as the Bridegroom. In the fifth century, St. Augustine said the Cross is the marriage bed upon which Jesus consummated His marriage to His Bride, the Church.[3] It was on the Cross that our Lord expressed physically in and through His Body what He had already willed spiritually.

For most couples, the consummation of their marriage is something to be desired. They don't usually see it as a kind of crucifixion. But it's not the actual Crucifixion that a couple has to emulate. Rather, it's the love that caused our Lord to pour Himself out for us in His Crucifixion. It is true Jesus was troubled, knowing He was going to the Cross, yet He acknowledged this was the very reason He came to the hour of His Passion (John 12:27). He desired to go to the Cross, not only to take away our sins and reconcile us to God but also to show humanity—especially married couples—what love looks like in the lived reality. This is the disposition spouses must have toward each other, not only on the first occasion of their intimacy but on every occasion throughout their marriage.

As we have seen, love is selfless. In fact, the love vowed in marriage is a daily dying to self for the sake of one's spouse. Jesus required that we take up our crosses daily and follow Him (Luke 9:23). Due to the physical pleasure and psychological and emotional intensity involved in the marital act, it is very easy to be selfish. As we will address later, this act is the very expression of the marriage and the physical expression of the spiritual union that occurred at the moment the vows were professed and received.

In the book of Tobit (chapter 8) is a wonderful description of what this union should look like. A beautiful young woman named Sarah had been cursed by someone who desired her. If

---

[3]   St. Augustine, *Sermo Suppositus* 120:3.

a man married her with any selfish desires, a demon would kill him before the marriage could be consummated. Sarah had been married seven times, and each of her husbands was buried on the night of his wedding. Tobias desired her hand in marriage, and the archangel Raphael taught him how to break the curse and free Sarah from the oppression of the demon. On their wedding night, Sarah's father dug a grave for Tobias and then sent a maid to the bedroom to see if Tobias was still alive. Tobias, acting on the direction given him by St. Raphael, asked Sarah to get up and pray. Her father was amazed to see Tobias alive in the morning. What broke the curse? Obedience and charity.

The archangel Raphael gave Tobias a two-part cure to liberate Sarah. The first part got rid of the demon, and the second part broke the curse. The first part was purely external: to burn the heart of a fish. The second part required something internal and profound on the part of Tobias: to pray with Sarah on their wedding night. Tobias began their prayer with the creation of man and woman (vv. 5-6), which we considered in the first chapter. After calling upon the heavens and all creatures to bless God, Tobias came to the most profound part of his prayer and addressed the very purpose of the creation of the human person and of marriage: "And now, O Lord, I am not taking this sister of mine because of lust, but with sincerity. Grant that I may find mercy and may grow old together with her" (v. 7).

Tobias loved Sarah for who she was, not for what he could get from her. It was this pure love that broke the curse that had plagued Sarah, but this is also the kind of love that should be at the foundation of every marriage. Keep in mind, this was prior to our redemption. To be able to love this way, with the help of God's grace, can be very difficult, but even without the grace of a redeemed humanity, Tobias was able to love Sarah as human persons were created to love: solely for the good of the other. If there had been selfishness on the part of Tobias, he might have found himself in the grave his father-in-law had dug for him!

This is this same kind of pure love that sets us free from our slavery to sin. Recall that a sacramental marriage is not just the union of the couple but a union of the couple with God. In fact, God is the cause of the union. Because the sacrament is holy, the physical expression of the sacrament must be holy. It may seem unusual to think of the sexual union of a married couple as being holy, but the union of the bodies of a married couple is the physical expression of the spiritual union of their souls. The union of the souls is holy; therefore, the union of their bodies must also be holy.

On the day of their marriage, a couple asks God to unite their souls in Holy Matrimony. God does not disappear from the relationship just because the sacrament has been confected. No, God is still very much at the center of the marriage of every couple who are in the state of grace. God cannot be excluded from any part of the marriage; this means He should not be excluded from the intimacy of the couple. Indeed, if a couple wants greater intimacy, they should pray more, both as a couple and alone with God. The deeper their spiritual union, the deeper will be the intimacy of their physical union.

This also implies that the act of intercourse in marriage should be a kind of prayer. After all, prayer is simply about loving God, not about what we can get from God. In the previous chapter, we said that married persons should love their spouses in God and love God in their spouses. Seen this way, every action within marriage, especially in the act that expresses the marriage, should be an act of love and, therefore, a prayer.

If prayer (and marriage) is about loving, and loving is about seeking only the good of the other, then each spouse must be seeking only the good of the other in the act of intimacy. In other words, marital intimacy is not about selfish pleasure-seeking, because that would be using the other, not loving the other. Each spouse should have the disposition of saying, "I want this for the good and pleasure of my spouse." We can go even further to say: "I want this to be the most wonderful, pleasurable, beautiful experience of love my spouse has ever had."

Several times we have said that love is about giving and receiving. In marriage, both spouses give themselves completely to the other, and both receive completely what the other gives. While this is the disposition that should be operative in every aspect of a marriage, it is most critical in a couple's physical intimacy. While each must have the desire only for the good and pleasure of the other, it is also necessary for each to keep the heart open to receive the good—the pleasure—the spouse is giving.

Indeed, part of the gift you give is to receive the gift your spouse is giving you. Think of it this way. What if your spouse were to look at you and say: "I don't want anything from you. I just want this for your pleasure"? If your intention is to give to your spouse, then your gift is being rejected. This is why part of the gift you give to your spouse is to receive with love the gift your spouse is giving you.

This disposition is what will make the physical union the most beautiful. I suspect we all, when we were young, had the experience of taking something we were not supposed to take. Let's say, for instance, that you stole a cookie to eat secretly. You had very high expectations of the pleasure you would get from that cookie, and although it tasted good, it did not come close to meeting your expectations. On the other hand, if your mom unexpectedly offered you a cookie, well, a cookie never tasted so good.

Now apply this same thing to marital intimacy. If you are using your spouse, taking selfishly or seeking your own pleasure, there will still be pleasure, but it will not come close to meeting your expectations. This pleasure will be at the expense of your spouse rather than being a gift received from your spouse. But if you are not seeking anything for yourself, but seeking only to give in love to your spouse, then the gift you receive from your spouse will be well beyond anything you might have desired.

So we see here a distinction between taking and receiving. Taking is active; receiving is passive. Taking is using the other person; receiving is loving the other person. Spouses are to love one another. To take from the other is to use one's spouse as an object. To use, or to take, is the opposite of loving. Both spouses are created to love and to be loved. Both spouses have vowed to love each other. To give and to receive is both acting according to one's own dignity and treating one's spouse according to his or her dignity. Anything less is a violation of the dignity of both spouses and a violation of what each spouse vowed on the day of their marriage.

The giving of which we are speaking is a total self-gift. It is a dying to self in order to live for the other. One spouse dies to self and gives himself or herself to the other, and the other receives new life from his or her spouse. In other words, the spouses simultaneously experience the pouring out of their own lives into the other and the receiving of the other's life into themselves.

We see here another aspect of the holiness of the marital act: it is a sacrifice. The word *sacrifice* means "to make holy." So, following the example of Jesus the Bridegroom on the Cross, both spouses immolate themselves, and both spouses receive new life from the other. This experience of a kind of death and resurrection helps us to understand what Jesus meant when He said that whoever would save his life will lose it, but whoever loses his life for His sake will save it (Matt. 10:39). The psalmist speaks of the sun, which comes forth like a bridegroom leaving his chamber (Ps. 19:4–5). Like the life-giving rays of the sun, this bridegroom does not come forth as a conqueror. Rather, this bridegroom can only refer to a young man who has just given his life to his bride and has, for the first time, experienced the joy and glory of receiving new life from his wife.

This brings us back to the beginning of creation, when God put the man into a deep sleep and created the woman from his side. The man dies to self to give life to the woman. The woman receives life from the man and gives it back to him so that he, in turn, receives life from the woman. Both give, and both receive. Both die to self and rise to new life. This is the new creation following the pattern of death and resurrection established by our Lord on the Cross.

As we have seen, we are a new creation only by participating in the death and Resurrection of the Lord through Baptism. In marriage, the couple expresses this mystery in their day-to-day life and particularly in their physical intimacy

We saw earlier that everything in marriage is to be an act of love; everything is to be a prayer. Putting our focus, as we have been, on the conjugal union is good and important, but the physical intimacy of a couple is a microcosm of their entire relationship. A couple can look at their intimate life and see the reflection of their entire relationship. If their intimacy is selfish, the couple will see that selfishness reflected in other aspects of their marriage. If their intimacy is truly loving, they will see that selfless love reflected in the entirety of their relationship.

This is not only an important insight, but it is critical to the couple's marriage. All too often, couples are dissatisfied with their sexual lives and try all kinds of things to improve it. Frequently, men think that if they and their wives would have sexual relations more often, it would solve the problems in the marriage. Actually, just the opposite is true.

Recall that a marriage relationship consists of four basic aspects: communicational, relational, spiritual, and physical. The physical aspect of the marriage is the last aspect to address because, in most situations, it will reflect what is happening in the rest of the marriage. Work on the other areas of the marriage first, and the physical part of the marriage will follow; work on the physical aspect first, and it will not positively affect anything else. Usually, the attempt to "improve" the sexual part of the marriage will be selfish, and so, rather than helping the marriage, it will only cause further problems.

This brings us back to the point that was addressed earlier about prayer life. If marriage is first and foremost a spiritual union, what are you doing to build up the spiritual aspect of your marriage? Your soul and your spouse's soul were united on the day you were married. What are you doing to strengthen that spiritual union? If the physical aspect of the marriage expresses the spiritual aspect, then work on your spiritual life both individually and as a couple, and you will see a real improvement in the physical part of your relationship. Prayer will help you to love more and will conform you to Jesus, both in His dispositions and in His death and Resurrection.

We have already seen how these dispositions need to be central to a marital relationship, so more love and more dying to self will positively affect the way a couple treats each other, the way they communicate with each other, and the way they experience intimacy with each other. Remember the conversation I mentioned in the second chapter when one husband said to another: "If you think having relations with your wife is intimate, try praying with her." The spiritual intimacy experienced in prayer will carry over into a deeper and more profound intimacy in the physical union of the couple.

It has been said that the eyes are the window to the soul. God, who created human persons in love and gave them the great dignity of participating in His creative work through an act of love shared by a couple who have vowed to love each other, has given human couples a way to unite in both body and soul in the conjugal act. Of all the physical creatures God made, human persons are the only ones who look at each other in the act of procreation. So the couple can literally see the love of the other person in and through his or her eyes while they feel that love in their bodies.

The act of intercourse should be a physical re-pronunciation of your marriage vows—that is, a total and complete giving of yourself to your spouse as a gift and the total and complete receiving of your spouse's gift of self to you. Think back to the day you were married, when you looked each other in the eyes and made your vows. Wouldn't it make sense that the re-pronunciation of those vows, the physical expression of your vows, should be done in the same way? If the eyes are the window to the soul and the soul comprises a mind and a will (for truth and love), then looking into the soul through the eyes of one's spouse will help to guarantee that the sexual act is an act of true love. It is hard to look someone in the eye when lying to the person, so to say "I love you" while using the person does not work. You cannot hide the eyes.

If the intimacy within marriage is to be about love, and love is doing what is best for the other, then each person has to be aware of what is truly best for one's spouse. We live in a time when people are trying to claim that there are no real differences between men and women except for a few body parts. At the same time, psychologists can write books about the differences between men and women. The area of intimacy is one of the areas where the differences are vast. Because many couples do not discuss the aspects of their intimate life with each other, both may be easily frustrated when their needs are not being met.

As mentioned earlier, in many areas of the relationship, men treat their wives as if they were dealing with another man, and women treat their husbands as if they were dealing with another woman. The area of intimacy is no different. Each spouse often does for the other what he or she would want done for himself or herself. Each thinks he or she is giving the other what is best because it reflects his or her own desires. Unfortunately, this does not work. There is an adage that says: "Men will love in order to get sex; women will have sex in order to get love." Sadly, there is a lot of truth in this. I say "sadly" because, for both partners, it is not a loving attitude but a selfish one.

The needs of men are pretty obvious, but the needs of a woman are not so clear. For instance, what is important to a woman is affection: women want to be hugged, caressed, kissed, and so forth. Romance is also important for many women. Men, on the other hand, do not care as much about these things; they are focused more on the parts of the body dealing directly with sexuality. Consequently, women tend to caress their husbands, whereas men tend to move immediately to fondling and heavy petting. Women get frustrated because men want to move so quickly; men get frustrated because women take so much time to get aroused. When I talk with couples, I tell them that the arousal time for men is about two seconds, whereas for women it is about forty-five minutes. This means men have to be patient, but it also means they have to die to self to meet the needs of their wives.

I remember seeing a video of a woman who was giving a talk to married couples. Unfortunately, I do not have any reference to give her proper credit. She talked about some of the differences between men and women, including the present topic. She spoke about how men act toward their wives—that is, fondling and petting—and she said: "If you knew how much we hate that." The women in the audience applauded vigorously. She went on to say: "Don't touch us there until we beg you to touch us there." Once again, the women were vociferous in their agreement. She then talked about how women approach their husbands and explained how men care little about being caressed and hugged; she then told women to focus on just one area of her husband's body. The men in the audience loudly approved. Both need to pay attention to what this woman was saying, and both need to adjust themselves to the needs of the other.

One thing I hear over and over again is that women are frustrated with the intimacy in their marriage but will not say anything to their husbands. When I ask why they do not tell their husbands, the answer is always something along the line of, "I don't want to hurt him." If a man truly loves his wife, he wants to serve her. He wants what is best for her. If she is frustrated, he wants to make adjustments to please her. The problem is that if he sees she is frustrated but she does not tell him what she needs, he will assume he must not be doing enough and will try harder at what he has been doing. The result is that the woman will feel even worse.

Because the differences are so great in this area, it is necessary for a couple to discuss together how they can best serve one another. There's no generic template for this. Every person is different, so what one person finds exciting might do nothing for another. The intimacy between a couple is truly unique to that couple. But there are general patterns in the way men and women approach intimacy that are useful to bear in mind.

For instance, women, being relational, will notice something is not right and will try to figure out how to remedy the problem.

If what they try does not work, they go (figuratively speaking) to their kitchen drawer and try a different utensil. If that does not work, they will go back and try again and again until they find something that works. Men, on the other hand, show up for the job with just one tool. If they have pliers when they need a wrench, they will try and try to make the pliers work. If, after turning them backward and upside down, the pliers do not work, the man will put them down and walk away.

For most women, it sounds like a put-down to tell her husband what she needs. If she were dealing with another woman, it would be looked at negatively. Not so with a man. He won't be offended if a woman tells him what she needs. After all, if he knows beforehand, he can arrive with the right tool for the job. It will actually be a great relief for the man to know the wants and needs of his wife.

A woman might object that it would be selfish to tell her husband what she needs and that it would be more charitable to accept what he is giving. It would be selfish if it were done merely for the sake of what she could get. However, if a wife tells her husband what she needs in order to help him meet her needs, then she's actually performing an act of charity. Any man who truly loves his wife wants to please her. Not knowing how to please his wife will frustrate him and leave his wife frustrated as well because her needs will not be met. If she tells her husband in charity what she needs, the frustration of both can disappear.

The sexual union of the couple is the sign of their marital union. The ring on the finger is a sign to everyone else that a person is married, but the actual sign of the sacramental marriage is shared only between the two spouses. When I was teaching seniors in high school, every year I was asked why two young people who are "in love with each other" cannot engage in sexual relations. I would answer this question from several perspectives, but it finally came down to the point of what the sexual union is. It is the sign of marriage, and if the two people are not married, their union would be a lie. They would be trying to express something that does not exist.

Invariably, there would be some pushback, so I would use the example of another sacrament. I would ask the young people: "What if, on Sunday morning, the priest woke up with a horrible case of the stomach flu? Could we call one of the seminarians to say Mass?" "Of course not," they would answer. Then I would ask if we could call one of the transitional deacons to say Mass, since they would soon be ordained priests. When they would answer that a deacon could not say Mass, I would ask, "Why not?" The young people would answer, "Because they are not priests." To which I would respond: "And you are not married, so you cannot not do what is reserved for marriage." I would explain that a seminarian is like a person who is dating and a transitional deacon is like a person who is engaged. Mass is the highest expression of the priesthood, and no one can offer Mass unless he is a priest. The sexual union of a couple is the highest expression of their marriage, and no one can engage in this act of intimacy unless they are married. Outside of marriage, any attempt to engage in any kind of sexual activity is a sin because it's selfish. More than that, it's a lie. Anyone who engages in sexual activity outside of marriage is trying to express something that does not exist.

This brings us to an important point for those who were not chaste with one another prior to being married. As we have demonstrated, any sexual activity (not just fornication or adultery) outside of marriage is a mortal sin. When a couple establishes an intimate relationship before marriage, this can cause some practical problems after they are married. Once the pattern of a sexual relationship is established, it is very difficult to switch gears and change the parameters of the relationship. In other words, it is very difficult for two people who are acting selfishly and using each other before marriage to say suddenly, "We are married now, so we will no longer use each other. From now on, this will be an act of love." In this situation, a couple will need to talk deeply with each other, to determine what needs to change, and to make an act of the will to make the necessary changes.

Most people do not consider another aspect of premarital relations. When a couple sins against each other prior to marriage, they are telling each other that it is acceptable to them if the other person violates the Sixth Commandment. However, the unspoken stipulation is this: "It is okay for you to violate the Sixth Commandment, but only with me." If a relationship is established on infidelity to God, why would one person expect the other person to be faithful to him or her? This is why it is necessary to require responsibility and true charity prior to marriage; both are demonstrated in chastity. If someone demonstrates charity and chastity before marriage, there is good reason to assume that that person will be loving and faithful in marriage. If the person pushes for sexual intimacy prior to marriage, how can one expect him or her to be responsible and faithful after being married? If a husband was selfish *before* the wedding, when he was trying to win his wife's hand, the selfishness will carry right into the marriage and into the intimacy within the marriage. In many marriages, one of the spouses (usually the woman) wakes up one morning a short time after getting married and wonders if she made the biggest mistake of her life. Purity in mind and body are necessary on a number of levels.

Everything mentioned above about the problems caused by a lack of chastity prior to marriage can be applied with even greater emphasis to a married couple who is practicing contraception in any form. Contraception will immediately and automatically turn the sexual relationship into something selfish. The union of the couple is intended to be the sign and expression of the marriage, the expression of total self-giving. To employ any form of contraception means the couple will go through the motions of offering themselves as a sacrifice but then fail to give the gift. What does it say about a couple's understanding of their marriage if they refuse to give themselves totally to each other?

The promised allure of contraception is "pleasure without responsibility." Unfortunately, there is also the promise of sex without love and "love" without life. This does not imply that there is no love between the couple. However, they are not acting with purity of love—with true charity—as they vowed on the day of their marriage. If we look more in depth at this situation, we find that contraception involves a threefold violation:

1. It is a violation of the marriage vows. The vows were to love each other. Instead, the couple is using each other. This makes contraception a lie, or a violation of truth.

2. It is a violation of the persons involved because the persons are made to love and be loved, but now they are neither loving nor being loved. So contraception is a violation of love.

3. Contraception, which means "against conception," is a violation of the very purpose of human sexuality in both the love-giving and the life-giving aspects. The couple is failing not only to love each other but also to die to self and give life to the other. And, of course, there is a rejection of the openness to new life as well. So contraception is a violation of life.

Ultimately, using contraception is a choice against God and one's own dignity as a person created in the image and likeness of truth, love, and life! Tragically, the choice to use contraception is usually based on ignorance, often willful ignorance.

In 1968, Pope St. Paul VI wrote an encyclical letter titled *Humanae Vitae*. It's one of the most maligned documents in the history of the Church because it upholds the Church's two-thousand-year-old teaching about the dignity of the human person and human sexuality and, therefore, upholds the Church's teaching that contraception is a grave sin. Because of this teaching, many people have said the Church is stuck in the Middle Ages or needs to "get into the twenty-first century."

If you have not read *Humanae Vitae*, I strongly urge you to do so. The document is only fifteen pages long, but it's packed with important teachings. For our purposes, these teachings include the four characteristics of conjugal love: it is fully human, total, and faithful until death, and fecund. *Humanae Vitae* teaches that the unitive and procreative aspects of marriage cannot be separated. It also teaches that the social consequences of contraception will be fourfold: a road open to conjugal infidelity, a general lowering of morals, men losing respect for women, and public authorities taking no heed of moral requirements. When we consider these consequences, we see that rather than being stuck in the Middle Ages, the Church was in the twenty-first century more than thirty years before the twenty-first century arrived. What Pope St. Paul VI stated would happen has all come to pass. *Humanae Vitae* not only presents Church teaching; it has proven to be truly prophetic.

Having said all this, it might be helpful to provide some history on the subject of contraception. The Church has condemned contraception in all its forms right from the beginning. Every Protestant denomination condemned contraception until 1930 (vulcanized rubber, and thus condoms, were invented in the 1920s). In that year, the Anglicans held their decennial Lambeth Conference, where it was determined that contraception was acceptable in difficult situations. If it is acceptable for one difficult situation, it is acceptable for all situations. Every Protestant denomination quickly signed on to this concession, allowing contraception for anyone. In 1930, Pope Pius XI wrote an encyclical letter titled *Casti Connubii* (Chaste wedlock) which reaffirmed the Church's constant teaching. This document left the Catholic Church as the only major voice in the world speaking in favor of the dignity of marriage and married love and against contraception. It is also worth noting that, beginning in the 1920s, with the invention of each new form of contraception, the divorce rate jumped. Forms of contraception were available to more and more people. This continued into the 1960s, when the contraceptive pill was introduced and the divorce rate increased to 55 to 60 percent, where it has remained ever since. The only major change in the dynamics of marriage was contraception.

Protestant supporters of contraception (as well as Catholic critics of *Humanae Vitae*) ask, "Where is contraception condemned in the Bible?" Contraception is condemned in a number of places in Scripture. The first is in Genesis 38, when, during intercourse, a man named Onan withdraws and ejaculates outside of the woman (v. 9). God was displeased, and Onan died. To this day, this sin still bears his name. Beyond this, every time witchcraft or sorcery is mentioned in the Bible, it is about contraception. The Greek word *pharmakeia* is translated in the New Testament as "sorcery" (see Gal. 5:20; Rev. 9:21; 18:23; 21:8; 22:15). The ancients knew that some plants and potions could be used as contraceptives or would cause miscarriages, but only a witch or a sorcerer (*pharmakos*) made and sold contraceptive potions. So when witchcraft and sorcery are condemned in the Bible, contraception is also being condemned.

The Church speaks about the necessity for marriage and sexuality to be fully human. This means that sexuality envelops the entire person, endowed with an intellect and a free will. Therefore, the Church allows couples to use their intellects in order to understand the natural cycles of the woman's body and to use their wills to choose to engage in marital relations only in nonfertile times if there is need to avoid pregnancy. Many people immediately think of this as the "rhythm method." In fact, several forms of Natural Family Planning have been developed that are scientifically based and are as effective as hormonal and barrier contraceptive methods at postponing or avoiding pregnancy. These natural methods can help couples to achieve a pregnancy or to avoid pregnancy when there are serious reasons to do so. These serious reasons include a physical or psychological condition of the husband or wife that would cause great difficulties if a child were conceived, as well as external conditions such financial hardships. The Church allows Natural Family Planning but does not require it of couples. Each couple can choose what is right and best for them, as long as their decisions remain within the bounds of what is morally acceptable.

Some people call Natural Family Planning "Catholic contraception." This is not true. Contraceptives, if that is what they actually are, have as their intention to block the egg and the sperm from meeting. Some "contraceptives" are actually abortifacients, meaning that if a baby is conceived, they will prevent implantation. In other words, the newly conceived child will simply exit the womb. With Natural Family Planning, the egg and the sperm arrive at the same place but at different times. Nothing prevents their meeting, nor does anything prevent implantation if conception occurs.

Pope Paul VI said that the unitive and procreative aspects of marital acts cannot be separated. We have looked in a variety of ways at the unitive aspect of the conjugal embrace. The two become one in the sacrament of Holy Matrimony, and this unity is expressed physically in the sexual union of the couple. We have also discussed the necessity of ensuring that this act is truly an act of love. Of course, it is also through this act that children are conceived. This is the procreative aspect of the act. The Church does not say that a couple must intend to conceive each time they engage in marital relations; she says that nothing can be put in the way to prevent the possibility of a new life being conceived.

The Church has several reasons for this teaching. First, it is in keeping with what was vowed in the marriage. Pope Paul VI emphasizes that conjugal love must be total. When the vows were made, both spouses gave their entire person—with all their potential—to the other, holding nothing back. If the marital union is the physical expression of the vows, then this union must be a total self-giving, including the potential for parenthood. As we saw earlier, to put something in the way of conception would be going through the motions but failing to give the total gift of self. Spouses who use contraception are using each other because they are rejecting some aspects of the other person's gift of self.

Second, love is always life-giving. If a couple causes a barrier to be placed between them, the sexual act is not life-giving for one another. They are not dying to self; they are not pouring out their life for the other. Therefore, neither are they experiencing the resurrection or the new life of the other being poured into themselves. As we saw in chapter 1, love overflows any boundaries we can put on it. This means that if a couple is truly loving each other, their love will necessarily overflow the boundaries of the two of them. This overflow of love becomes life-giving for others, whether that be a child who is conceived or others who receive their service. To place any restrictions on the marital act is to say that the love remains only between the two and goes no further. This is a denial of the very nature of love and a violation of the persons, both of whom are made for love.

Third, if a child is conceived, the child should be conceived in love. The "failure rate" of contraceptives means that a number of children are conceived in acts of selfishness and lust. There was no desire for a child, and there was no true openness to life, so the child who is conceived is living in a contradiction of sorts: being created *for* love, but not being created *in* love. Children should be the fruit of love. As we have seen, a couple should be able to see the love they have for one another in the beautiful face of their child. What will they see when they know they were not acting in love when the child was conceived? This is why the Church requires every marital act to be fecund, or open to life.

The Church's teaching regarding contraception is not only for the good of marriage in general but is also of the greatest importance for women. By this I do not mean merely the many adverse effects that contraceptives have on women's health and psychological well-being, though such effects are well documented. Rather, I am speaking more about the importance for a woman in the marital relationship. When contraceptives are involved, the intimacy in the relationship tends to become focused on only the sexual act, to the exclusion of the affection that is so necessary for a woman. When a couple chooses to abstain rather than to contracept, they need to find other ways of expressing their affection that will not lead them into intercourse. Once again, each couple is unique, so what might be a good form of affection for one couple might cause arousal in another. Each couple needs to work together to find these ways of expressing love and affection outside of the sexual act itself.

This brings up another frequently asked question: "Once we are married, can we do anything we want sexually?" Considering this question from the objective point of morality first, there is one overarching principle: ejaculation must always be vaginal. For the woman, climax must always be in the context of intercourse. In other words, since the woman may not experience a climax during intercourse, her husband can bring her to a climax right before or after the act of intercourse. It is not permissible to intentionally cause either of the spouses to achieve an orgasm outside of the context of intercourse. To do so would be a mortal sin. Also, it is not permissible for the woman to cause the orgasm herself, because that would be an act of masturbation. This is where a conscientious husband needs to be aware of his wife's needs and be determined to provide for those needs.

To consider this question from a practical perspective, the Church teaches that it is permissible for a couple to engage in any foreplay activities up to and including beginning the act of intercourse and stopping prior to ejaculation. This being said, several points need to be considered. First of all, as mentioned above, the couple has to know what will lead them to arousal and what will not. Although morally a couple can begin the act of intercourse, then stop and go to sleep, from a practical perspective, one has to ask if that is humanly possible. Also, in God's design, all aspects of foreplay are intended to lead a couple to the completion of the marital embrace. If this is the case and the couple is not planning to engage in marital relations, the couple needs to know what they can do that will not lead to arousal or at what point they are able to stop.

Second, although there are a variety of acts that are morally acceptable, each spouse, and the couple together, must determine what is and is not appropriate. Two questions can be asked: (1) Is this in keeping with my spouse's dignity? (2) If I truly love this person, would I ask him or her to perform this act? This being said, it should also be obvious that one cannot force one's spouse to do something that he or she does not want to do. In his Letter to the Hebrews, St. Paul instructs couples to keep the marriage bed undefiled; then he speaks of the immoral and adulterous who will be judged by God (Heb. 13:4). Certainly, St. Paul is referring to maintaining proper chastity within the marriage, but I think this can also be applied to the intimacy between the couple. Always act out of true charity for the other, because love never wrongs the beloved.

Another aspect of charity, chastity, and fidelity in marriage that must be addressed is pornography. Men, as mentioned above, are visual and physical by nature. Therefore, pictures and videos of women or sexual acts are very powerful for them. Women, on the other hand, are more imaginative and relational; therefore, women are attracted to things such as romance novels. This point needs to be stressed: steamy romance novels do to women what pornography does to men. For both, it is destructive in the marital relationship. For both, it is really infidelity to the vows made on the day of marriage. In their marriage vows, each person gave everything to the other and made a promise of fidelity. Each person gave the other his or her body and soul, including his or her imagination, which is part of the intellect. To look at another lustfully or to imagine something romantic with another person is a violation of what was vowed. Looking at pornography or engaging in impure fantasies are mortal sins for anyone, but they have a greater gravity for people who are married because of the vows they professed.

These sins cause particular problems in the marital intimacy because one's spouse is not the focus of love. Rather, the person is often using his or her spouse to act out a fantasy. If one's spouse is not enough to get a person aroused, then there is a crisis of love in the relationship that must be addressed.

The vast majority of pornography is directed toward men, which is why women are presented as objects. All women are created equal in dignity, so a man cannot look at one woman as an object and then think he can look at his wife as a person endowed with dignity, made for love. What's more, the person involved in pornography still has dignity, even if that person does not know it or accept it.

If a couple is working to truly love one another, they will know immediately if they are being used. Women are usually more sensitive to this, but a man who is focused on loving his wife will pick up on it as well. If one spouse is looking at pornography or engaging in any other activities that violate the marriage covenant, the other spouse will know it by the way he or she is approached and acted on. Because they have experienced real love in the relationship, if there is something selfish or lustful, they will immediately notice the shift in the relationship.

Most often, looking at pornography is not an end in itself. It almost always leads to occasions of masturbation. This, too, is a mortal sin because it violates one's own dignity. If a person is married, the sin becomes even greater because it is a violation of the marriage vows and an attempt to take back something that has been given away. The sexual faculties are given by God to be given to another person in marriage. This means the sexual faculties are for another person's pleasure, not one's own selfish pleasure. To try to use the sexual faculties for one's own pleasure is therefore a violation of those faculties, of one's own dignity, of the vows made in marriage, and of the spouse, to whom the faculties were given in the sacrament of Matrimony.

More and more women are starting to look at pornography that involves other women. Most of the time, this is done to compare themselves with the women being pictured. Once again, the women in these images are not being treated with dignity; they are being violated. Women who look at pornography to compare themselves with the women being portrayed also violate their own dignity and usually perceive themselves as less desirable or attractive than the women in the images. All of this is serious sin.

Sadly, many couples watch pornographic and other sexually explicit movies together. This kind of activity will result in a severe deformation of their marriages and their marital intimacy. What is being portrayed in these movies or videos has no relation to intimacy in a marriage. These movies not only present sexuality in a way that is gross and twisted, but they also promote selfishness in both persons. Looking at pornography is a mortal sin; moreover, the actions that follow from it are even worse. The couples who watch these movies often try to imitate what they are watching. It is usually degrading and cannot be equated with what occurs within the intimate relationship of a couple. Not only do external differences exist between them, but there is a 180-degree internal difference. It is lust, not love.

Jesus consummated His marriage to the Church in an act of total self-giving. Having poured Himself out so His Bride could receive His life, He stated: "*Consummatum est!*" This is the pure love, the charity, a couple vow to each other on the day they are united in the sacrament of Holy Matrimony, the day when they are also united to the mystery of the union of Christ and the Church. For this reason, a husband and wife who are called to love each other and to make each other saints will always reject anything contrary to love — not only because it is false but because it violates the dignity of the person with whom they are completely in love. Only spouses who have this kind of love for each other will understand the depth and beauty of our Lord's words spoken from His marriage bed.

Questions for Reflection

1. Do you think of making love with your spouse as an act of prayer? Does your physical intimacy bring you closer to each other spiritually?

2. When you and your spouse make love, are you conscious and respectful of each other's dignity? Do you engage in any behavior that is beneath your dignity?

3. Do you consume any media that may cause impure thoughts or corrupt your sexual relationship with your spouse (e.g., pornography, inappropriate movies, salacious novels)?

4. Every couple goes through a "dry spell." How may couples rekindle their intimate love while remaining generous and self-giving?

5. Are there any barriers between you and your spouse that prevent you from having a more pleasing, fulfilling relationship? Are you willing to have an open, honest, and charitable conversation with your husband or wife about those barriers?

6

You Are the Temple

We have already seen that the Bride of Christ and the Body of Christ are one and the same. However, the notion of the sacrificial love offered by the Church requires us to consider one additional aspect of the mystery of the Mystical Christ. Recall what our Lord said regarding His body: "Destroy this temple, and in three days I will raise it up" (John 2:19). St. John tells us He was speaking about His body (John 2:21). If His body is a temple, then the Church, the Body of Christ, is a Temple.

So the Church is Bride, Body, and Temple. It's within this Temple that the sacrifice of Christ is offered, and it's from within the Temple of the Church that the new life of grace is poured into the souls of those who are members of the Mystical Body of Christ and the life of grace is brought into the world.

Each of us is a member of the Church, a member of the Bride of Christ, a member of the Mystical Body of Christ, and a member of the Temple of Christ. St. Peter tells us that we are to be living stones built into a spiritual house (1 Pet. 2:5). Although each of us is a member of this Temple, each of us is also a temple of Christ in our own person. St. Paul teaches: "Do you not know that you are God's temple and that God's Spirit dwells within you?" (1 Cor. 3:16). How can one be both a temple and a member of a Temple?

Put it this way. We know that each family forms what is called a "domestic church." Your family is part of the universal Church; your family also *is* a church. In a similar manner, because of your Baptism, you are both a member of the Temple and a temple yourself. Because of your sacramental marriage, which is built on your Baptism, your family members are members of the Church, and your family is a domestic church.

This situation can be made simpler if we apply the Greek terms for *temple*. In Greek, two words are used for temple: *hieron* is the word for the large temple or holy place, whereas *naos* is the word for a small temple or a shrine. With this distinction, we can consider the family, the domestic church, in comparison with the parish church. For the sake of our comparison, think of your parish church as the *hieron* (the large temple) and your family as the *naos* (the small temple).

Before we discuss the relationship between the large temple and the small temple, it makes sense to consider first the purpose of a temple. The temple is a place of worship. Many temples are dedicated to false gods. Within these temples, false gods are worshiped, and sacrifices are offered to them. For the Jewish people, there was to be only one Temple, which was ultimately built in Jerusalem. It was in the Jerusalem Temple that God dwelt among His people. People would go to the Temple to pray, worship, and offer sacrifice. After the death and Resurrection of Christ, the worship of the one true God was no longer limited to the city of Jerusalem (see John 4:21–24). The Church is the New Jerusalem, so wherever the Church is, there is Jerusalem. This means that every parish church is a place where God dwells among His people, as

He does in the Eucharist. Each church is consecrated to God and is therefore a holy place. Each church is a place where people can pray and seek union with God. It is a place where the sacrifice of the New Covenant is offered.

On the day you were baptized, you became a temple of the Lord. As a temple, you are the dwelling place of God (see John 14:23), and the Holy Spirit dwells within you (see 1 Cor. 3:16). As a temple in which God dwells, you are to pray and seek union with God in your heart. As a temple, you are called to offer sacrifice in union with the sacrifice of Jesus.

When you were baptized, you were consecrated to God. At that moment, God sealed you with an indelible mark. This mark or seal consecrates you for divine worship and special service in the Church. In Baptism, you were made holy through the infusion of sanctifying grace. When a person is in the state of grace, that person is holy. This is all so beautiful and amazing, but it becomes even more beautiful when a Christian couple enters into the union of marriage!

From the beginning, married life and love were to reflect the holiness and life of the Most Holy Trinity. However, God was not satisfied with marriage being merely a reflection of the Trinity. He brought it much deeper into the divine life by connecting the mystery of the marriage of Christ and the Church with the mystery of the marriage of a man and a woman. When two baptized persons enter into a sacramental marriage, the two become one. Each baptized person is a temple of the Lord, but one of the fruits of this union of persons in Holy Matrimony is that because the two become one, the couple become one temple, one body. Each spouse is a temple, and together they are a new temple, the domestic church. As we have seen, this union is holy. God unites the couple, so He is present with them and within them when they are in the state of grace. Therefore, marriage is a place of sacrifice and worship in honor of the one true God. Marriage is also a place of prayer in which the couple seeks union with God and a deeper union with each other.

Let's continue with our comparison of the parish church as the *hieron* and the domestic church as the *naos*. Your parish church is a beehive of activity. However, within the church building, three places have the greatest importance. The tabernacle, where our Lord is present, is certainly the greatest of the great. The other two places of prominence are the baptismal font and the altar. These three places in the church building are where the most important parish activities occur. What is interesting is that although the activities associated with these three places in the church are the most important, the amount of time spent at these locations is relatively small when compared with the other activities that fill the day. If this is true in the parish church, then we should find something similar in the domestic church.

Likewise, we should find God in the most prominent spot in the temple of ourselves. Indeed, He is found in the heart (spiritually, not physically) of every person who is in the state of grace. If we are not in the state of grace, we have ushered God out of His own temple. God is also found in the most prominent place in the marriage, which is in the union of the couple's souls. It is He who unites the souls of a married couple and maintains that unity. In other words, in the temple of a couple united in Holy Matrimony, God is present in the intimacy of the union of souls.

Our Lord's presence in the Eucharist is too often ignored by many people. He is present in the tabernacle so He can be with us and we can be with Him, so we can pray, grow in holiness, grow in love, and be transformed to become more and more like Him, in whose image and likeness we are made. Likewise, our Lord's presence in the temple of our bodies and in the new temple of the one body in marriage is also often ignored. Our Lord is dwelling here, too, because He wants to be with us so we can talk with Him, grow in love, and be more perfectly conformed to the three Persons of the Holy Trinity, who dwell within. When we are in union with Him, we find peace, we die to self, and we live for the other. In recognizing His presence within us and learning to receive His gift to us, married couples learn to receive the gift of their spouses, and as they learn to give themselves to the Lord, they learn to give themselves to their spouses.

Marriage, as has been shown several times, is, above all, a spiritual union. God unites the souls of you and your spouse in a spiritual bond, but you and your spouse must follow through with what you have asked of God. Having asked our Lord to be at the center of your marriage, it is now your task to make God the center of your marriage. He will not force Himself on you in any way. He created you with a free will; therefore, you must choose for yourselves what the priorities in your marriage will be. If God is your first priority, all other priorities will fall into proper position. But if God is not your first priority, the other priorities in your marriage will most often be misaligned. In his Letter to the Colossians, St. Paul describes the lived reality of the Christian life, specifically the life of the Christian family:

> Put on then, as God's chosen ones, holy and beloved, compassion, kindness, lowliness, meekness, and patience, forbearing one another and, if one has a complaint against another, forgiving each other; as the Lord has forgiven you, so you also must forgive. And above all these put on love, which binds everything together in perfect harmony. And let the peace of Christ rule in your hearts, to which

indeed you were called in the one body. And be thankful. Let the word of Christ dwell in you richly, as you teach and admonish one another in all wisdom, and as you sing psalms and hymns and spiritual songs with thankfulness in your hearts to God. And whatever you do, in word or deed, do everything in the name of the Lord Jesus, giving thanks to God the Father through him. (3:12–17)

Before addressing the points St. Paul makes in this passage, I want to emphasize that this teaching is directed at Christian families. I say this because, immediately following this passage from Colossians, St. Paul repeats what he taught married couples in his Letter to the Ephesians, and he also addresses children: "Wives, be subject to your husbands, as is fitting in the Lord. Husbands, love your wives, and do not be harsh with them. Children, obey your parents in everything, for this pleases the Lord" (Col. 3:18–20). In other words, this is how St. Paul envisions the day-to-day life of the domestic church.

St. Paul begins this passage by addressing his readers as chosen, holy, and beloved. Marriage is a vocation; you have been called and chosen by God. Jesus told His apostles: "You did not choose me, but I chose you" (John 15:16). The same is certainly true regarding the beautiful sacrament of Holy Matrimony. It is true that you and your spouse have chosen each other, but if you prayed about your vocation and trusted in the Lord, then He actually chose you and your spouse for each other and brought you together. As a temple of the Lord, you are holy and called to great holiness in union with God. You are loved by God with an everlasting love (see Jer. 31:3), a love that comes from God and gives you the ability to love Him in return and to love your spouse and others with the love you have received from God.

Following this description of your dignity, St. Paul goes on to teach how we are to act in accordance with our dignity and describes how we are to treat others according to their dignity. Although it would seem this should not be an issue in a marriage or in a family, we sometimes take one another for granted and treat people outside our own family with more respect than we treat the members of our own families. Most of what St. Paul says is self-explanatory, so I will not address each point individually. However, I would like to present some elements of the spiritual life that will help to put into practice the general principles St. Paul enumerates.

First and foremost is the necessity of prayer. Each person in the family needs to have his or her own spiritual life. The husband and the wife must pray together, and they should also bring the family together for prayer. Mental prayer, often known as contemplative prayer, is done alone. Even when a couple prays this kind of prayer together, each spouse is actually praying individually. Above all other forms of prayer, mental prayer brings us into union with the will of God. This is the prayer that changes our lives and helps us grow in virtue.

One form of prayer that can be done alone, as a couple, or as a family is the Liturgy of the Hours, the official prayer of the Church. This prayer is required of priests and consecrated persons and is prayed in monasteries. The Church encourages everyone to pray this prayer in part or completely. It is divided into seven "hours" or times during the day to pray. Some couples will pray Morning Prayer or Evening Prayer together; a couple might pray Night Prayer before going to bed. Reading Scripture is another form of prayer and an excellent way to fill one's mind with the Word of God. Praying the Rosary is a necessity each day. The Chaplet of Divine Mercy is given by our Lord Himself. Novenas can be prayed in preparation for a feast day or to ask some favor.

When possible, it is always best to go to a church or an adoration chapel for personal prayer. When this is not possible, it is most helpful to set aside a place in the home for prayer.

Of course, prayer for one another cannot be neglected. Prayer is the greatest work of charity, so praying for one another, especially for those in grave need, will help us to treat each other more charitably and dispose our hearts to be more willing and ready to forgive. Often, couples take each other for granted and forget or neglect to pray for each other. Such neglect can only be detrimental to your relationship.

Also, remember that, because a married couple is spiritually united, whatever one person does spiritually affects the other person. If one sins, the other spouse is not guilty of sin, but the sin of one spouse pulls the other down. At the same time, if one spouse does something that builds up the spiritual life, the other spouse is positively affected by that. Therefore, if one spouse can attend daily Mass, it will benefit both. Obviously, it is even better if both can attend daily Mass. If every day is not feasible, attending Mass even one or two days during the week will be of immense benefit to the individual, to the couple, and to the marriage.

Going to Confession on a regular basis is critical to our spiritual lives. It also helps us overcome vices and grow in virtue. Confession helps us to recognize our weaknesses and our dependence on the Lord. When we see how often we sin, Confession can also help us to be more compassionate and forgiving when others hurt us. St. Paul described the need to forgive as the Lord has forgiven us (Col. 3:13). We trust God to forgive us, but Jesus requires us to forgive others. Our Lord teaches this point many times in the Gospels, and we must keep in mind that in the Lord's Prayer, we ask God to forgive us only as much as we are willing to forgive others. So important is this teaching that it is the only petition in the Lord's Prayer that Jesus commented on, teaching us that if we do not forgive others, we will not be forgiven (Matt. 6:15).

We need to keep in mind two points regarding forgiveness. First, to forgive someone is not to say that whatever that person did was okay. God forgives us, but He will never say it was okay that we sinned. Second, it requires one to forgive, but it requires two to reconcile. This means we can always forgive others, even if they have not apologized or do not want to be reconciled. We cannot reconcile with others unless they are willing, but we can always forgive.

Returning to the places of importance in the *hieron*, the church building, the second place of importance is the baptismal font. The baptismal font is used only once in a person's lifetime. Each of us professes our baptismal vows only once (although these vows can be renewed many times). At the moment we are baptized, we are initiated into the New Covenant. St. Paul tells us that when we were baptized, we were baptized into the death of Christ so we can share in His Resurrection (Rom. 6:3–5). Sanctifying grace, the life of God, was infused into our souls, and we became partakers in the divine nature (2 Pet. 1:4). At that moment, the Holy Trinity began to dwell in our souls, making us temples of God, and we were incorporated into the Mystical Body of Christ. As members of Jesus Christ, we share in everything that He is; this means we share in His threefold office of priest, prophet, and king. We have spoken of these truths before, but they are repeated here because if this is the norm in the *hieron*, we should expect to find something similar in the *naos*, the small temple or shrine.

Indeed, in the domestic church we find correlations for each of these mysteries. The wedding ceremony is to the domestic church what the baptismal font is for the parish church. In marriage, a couple professes their vows only once, although these vows, too, may be renewed many times. At the moment the vows are professed and received, the couple is initiated into a covenant. In marriage, as we have said, each person dies to himself or herself and receives life from the other, so there is a death and a resurrection. In this giving of life to each other and receiving of life from each other, the couple shares in a new kind of life together. As we saw earlier, a shared dignity exists in this shared life, wherein the union of persons that was established by the Lord produces one new temple where He dwells within the union of souls.

At the moment the couple is married, they are incorporated into one another. In this new life of marriage, there must also be the means of expressing the baptismal offices of priest, prophet, and king. The office of the priest is the office of mediation and sacrifice. The office of the prophet is the office of the teacher. The office of the king is the office of service.

Before we address the exercise of the baptismal priesthood in expressing the sign of the marital covenant, let us consider the daily life of the parish priest. The primary activity of the life of the parish — and its priest — takes place at the altar. This action is the sacrifice of Jesus, the Bridegroom, for His Bride, the Church, and, as we saw earlier, it is also the Bride offering her life for and to her Bridegroom. In the Mass, Jesus is the *Priest* who offers the sacrifice to His Heavenly Father, the *Altar* on which the sacrifice is offered to God, and the *Victim* who is offered by the priest (acting *in Persona Christi*) as the sacrifice to God.

When a priest is ordained, a change takes place in his very being so the priest is able to stand *in Persona Christ* — that is, "in the Person of Christ." Jesus works through the humanity of the priest to confect the sacraments. As a man, a priest has no power to change bread and wine into God, nor has he the power in himself to forgive sins. Only God can do these things. Jesus is the Priest who works through the human priest to provide the sacraments for His people. We will consider each of these three aspects of the Mass—the priest, the altar, and the victim—as they apply to the domestic church.

The primary activity in the life of the parish church takes place at the altar, which is also central to the domestic church. In the temple of the domestic church, the wife is the altar and the husband is the priest of the family. In the union of the two, the bride and bridegroom both offer the sacrifice of themselves to and for the other. However, in the new temple forged by the marriage, there is only one offering. There is only one sacrifice because it flows from the union of the couple. The two become one, and together they offer one sacrifice. The two are united in their sacrifice; therefore, there are not two victims, but one. The wife exercises her baptismal priesthood as the altar in the domestic church; the husband exercises his baptismal priesthood as the priest serving at the altar. Both are united in exercising their baptismal priesthood as the victim or the lamb of sacrifice.

As in the parish church, so in the domestic church. There is one priest, one altar, and one victim.

In the Church today, thousands of priests minister at thousands of altars in thousands of churches around the world. Ultimately, there is only one Priest, one Altar, and one Victim: Jesus Christ. But to understand the dignity of what takes place in the sacrifice of marriage, it may be easier to use the sacrifices that took place in the Temple in Jerusalem as an example.

In Judaism, there was only one Temple, which was located in Jerusalem. In this one Temple, there was only one altar, at which only a true priest of God could offer sacrifice. There were many priests in Israel, but a man had to prove he was a priest before he could minister at the altar. On the other hand, throughout the ancient world, there were many temples and altars at which pagan priests could offer their sacrifices to false gods. Some of these altars dedicated to false gods were not even located in a temple: they were built in high places and used for making offerings to false gods. A true priest of God could not offer sacrifice on an altar dedicated to a false god, and a false priest could not offer sacrifice at the altar dedicated to the one true God. This means that the priest and the altar cannot be separated. An offering to the one true God required a true priest offering an acceptable sacrifice on the one true altar. Anything else was false and unacceptable.

In a married couple, the domestic church, God has made a temple, an altar, and a priest. The temple, as we have seen, is found in the union of the husband and wife joined together by God. There is only one priest (the husband) and one altar (the wife). Anything else is false. The offering must also be pure and unblemished. In other words, it must be conformed to truth, love, and life. This is the only kind of sacrifice that can be offered to the one true God, who united the couple in marriage and desires to be at the center of their marriage. What this means is that contraception, selfishness, abuse, force, using each other, or any other kind of violation of the dignity of the persons and the dignity of human sexuality causes the offering to be blemished and therefore unacceptable or, worse, offers it to a false god.

The couple's fidelity is required because there is only one altar and one priest in the one temple. Any attempt of a true priest to offer sacrifice on a false altar or any attempt of a false priest to offer sacrifice on the true altar would be a desecration. Such an offering is not a sacrifice; it is not a total self-gift; it is not holy. The temple, the altar, and the priest are all consecrated to God, but the only offering acceptable to the one true God is the one sacrifice of the couple united in love, offered on the one altar God has dedicated to Himself, and offered by the one priest authorized by God to minister at the one altar in His temple.

The sacrifice the couple offers must be a complete sacrifice — that is, the offering of their entire selves. The animal sacrifices of the Jewish people were holocausts, meaning that the victim was killed and then placed on the altar, where it was burned. It was a total sacrifice with nothing held back. As Catholics, we do not burn our sacrifices, but what we offer is still complete and total. At Mass, our sacrifice is Jesus, who offers Himself completely to the Father. This total sacrifice makes His offering a holocaust. Our Lord is sacrificed completely, but He is not put to death in the Mass. So His sacrifice at Mass is a "living holocaust." In a marriage, the sacrifice of the couple is also complete and total. Each person offers himself or herself totally to the other and, through the other, to God. Because each person dies to self without actually dying, the giving of one's entire life and person to the other also makes this sacrifice a living and life-giving holocaust.

In the New Testament, there is one Altar, one Priest, and one Victim: Jesus. In a sacramental marriage, each spouse is exercising his or her baptismal priesthood as a member of Christ, so in the marriage, there is only one altar, one priest, and one victim. St. Paul told us that the motive for marriage must always be charity. This, as we have seen, is the motive Jesus has in offering Himself to and for the Church, and this is the motive the Church has in offering herself to and for the Lord. If the motive for marriage is charity and the vow professed on the day of the marriage was charity, then the only proper motive for entering into the physical expression of the spiritual union of husband and wife is charity. If the motive is anything other than charity (that is, selfless love that seeks only the good of the other), then it is an act of selfishness. Being selfish, or going through the motions without love, is a lie.

It does not work. Externally, the appearance may be the same, but internally, it is backward. Rather than the priest making an offering to God, he is taking the gift for himself. Rather than the altar being the place of sacrifice, it becomes a place of desecration. When this happens, the very sign of the marriage is sullied. The priest fails to offer sacrifice, the altar is desecrated because it is being used for something other than offering sacrifice to God, and the temple becomes, as Jesus said, a "den of robbers" (Matt. 21:13). The couple is taking for themselves what is supposed to be offered as a sacrifice of charity to God and to each other. In such a situation, there is a true priest and a true altar within a true temple, but the victim is blemished and therefore unacceptable. It is not enough to go through the motions. The offering is made to God, who is truth and love; therefore, the offering must be made in truth and love.

We must always love in truth. Charity without truth is false. On the other hand, it is possible to have truth without charity, but truth without charity limps. It pushes away rather than attracts to itself. In the marital embrace, the two must be united in charity and in truth—that is, according to what was vowed on the day of their marriage. This means giving one's whole self to one's spouse, holding nothing back. It also implies receiving completely the gift of the other, neither rejecting any part of the gift or taking selfishly from the other.

Obviously, in a marriage, the victim is not killed. Rather, the two are giving their lives to and for each other. The totality of this offering, unlike when the victim is killed, includes not only the person as he or she is at the moment but also the potential of who the person can and will be. This potential encompasses the possibility of parenthood. The gift would not be total and complete if this potentiality, or any other potentiality in the persons or in the union of persons, were withheld. If anything is held back, the sacrifice is neither true nor loving and is therefore not a sacrifice acceptable to God. It is in violation of what was vowed on the day of the marriage. Recall that the word *sacrifice* means "to make holy." This means that the gift that is offered can be a sacrifice only when the priest and the altar are correctly performing the functions proper to each and, together, are offering the sacrifice to the Lord.

What would we think if the priest at Mass were being irreverent? What would we think if he took the focus off God and put it on himself? What would we think if he changed the words of consecration or used something other than bread and wine? Having seen the correlation of what happens in the parish church with what happens in the domestic church, what would we say about a husband and wife who were irreverent in their approach to each other? What would we think if they were selfish or self-seeking? What would we think if they removed God from the very act that expresses the union God Himself made? What would we think if the act were intentionally rendered infertile or impotent?

We would be—and should be—horrified if any of these things happened at Mass. Of course, if the words of consecration are changed or something other than bread and wine are used, the Mass is invalid. No sacrifice takes place. We should be equally horrified if a couple does not approach each other in a way that upholds their own dignity and the dignity of the other. If something is done intentionally to cause the act to be infertile or impotent, there is no sacrifice.

I think we can all agree that at Mass, the priest should approach the altar only with the greatest reverence and awe. In every convent chapel of the Missionaries of Charity, St. Teresa of Calcutta prominently placed a plaque where the priest would see it while he prepared for Mass. It reads: "Priest of God: Say this Mass as if it were your first Mass, your last Mass, your only Mass." If the priest followed this counsel, think of the reverence, the love, and the awe he would have as he offered the sacrifice of Jesus, and the sacrifice of himself as he acts in *Persona Christi*, to the Father. The sacrifice of a married couple should be characterized and governed by these same principles. They should approach each other as if it were the first time, the last time, the only time. Charity, respect, reverence, and awe should be the overriding factors each and every time a couple joins in love.

We have mentioned that the marital act, the mutual sacrifice of the couple, must always be complete. However, we need to reiterate the point that the couple does not need to have the intention of conceiving new life each time they engage in marital relations. Because the act expresses the total self-giving of each spouse to the other, nothing that would inhibit the potential of parenthood can be willfully or artificially placed in the way of that possibility. Even in those occasions where conception is either not intended or does not occur, new life is being given and received by the couple. Remember, a death and a resurrection take place: each spouse dies to self and gives that entire self to and for the other, and each spouse rises to new life by receiving the gift of the other's life, which is given in love. In the love that is given and received by the couple, a newness of life is experienced in both.

Again, consider the correlation with Mass at the parish church. The act that brings Jesus to the altar is the holiest act in the universe. The action of the Mass is the greatest expression of the love of Jesus, the Bridegroom, for His Bride, the Church. It is also the greatest expression of the love the Bride has for her Spouse.

The action that takes place in the *hieron* is the model for what occurs in the *naos*. The act that brings into the world a child, a human person, made in the image and likeness of God, is also holy.

Every act of marital intimacy should be the greatest expression of the love the couple has for each other and therefore needs to be approached and accomplished with the greatest love and reverence. This is true because of the dignity of the spouses, but even more when we consider that a child may be conceived as the fruit of this act. Life is the fruit of the marital embrace. It creates new life for each of the spouses and, possibly, new life in the person of a baby. Even if conception was not intended on a particular occasion and a baby is conceived, the baby is conceived according to the dignity of the spouses and the dignity of the child: in love, respect, reverence, and holiness. A child created in the image and likeness of God should be conceived when the parents are acting in the image and likeness of God. That way, even if the child was not intended at the moment of intimacy, the child is conceived in love and holiness and is accepted and loved in the same manner.

We spoke earlier of our participation in the threefold office of Jesus. Because we are baptized into Jesus, who is Priest, Prophet, and King, we also share in these offices. However, a means is required to participate in and exercise these offices fully. We said that the priestly office is one of mediation and sacrifice, the prophetic office is one of teaching, and the royal or kingly office is one of service. In the exercise of these three offices, we also see that the prophetic office is associated with truth, the royal office is associated with love, and the priestly office is associated with life. When a married couple properly expresses the sign of their marriage, the couple is able to exercise these offices and fulfill their dignity as members of Christ and persons made in the image and likeness of God—as persons made for truth, love, and life.

We have addressed the aspect of a couple being made by God into a new temple in their union of persons, but we have not clarified fully the aspects of the priest, the altar, and the victim.

Having seen how these operate in marriage, we need to consider each of these aspects in themselves.

In both Judaism and Catholicism, priesthood is reserved to males. While every person, male or female, who is baptized shares in the baptismal priesthood, the ministerial priesthood is reserved to men called by God. Being the head of a spiritual family, the priest is addressed with the title "Father." Within marriage and family life, only the man who is called by God to this august vocation is able to be the priest. As the head of his family, he also is graced with the title "Father." This title links him to the Fatherhood of God and informs his role in the family. He is to provide and to protect. He is to be creative. He is to love and serve.

As the priest in the family, he is to sacrifice himself for the sake of the others, thereby providing a place of stability and security for his wife, where children can be raised in peace and love. In his role as mediator, he must pray for each person entrusted to his care. He is to be the spiritual head of the family, bringing the family together for prayer and leading them in prayer. He must set the example of holiness, bringing his family to Mass and devotions, giving them the example of virtue.

The husband and father is to be a true Christian gentleman. Emphasis needs to be placed on *Christian*, but *gentleman* needs to be broken into its constitutive parts: he is to be a *gentle man*. He must be content with his own masculinity so that he uses it to serve others rather than to lord it over others. He is to be strong and decisive and yet gentle in his approach. All of this is necessary for a priest, but a priest is incomplete in himself. A priest needs an altar, and an altar needs a priest. Neither can fulfill the purpose of its existence without the other.

When it comes to offering the sacrifice of the Mass, the parish priest must prepare himself both spiritually and materially. By this I mean he must be properly disposed spiritually to offer the sacrifice of Christ to the Father. He must remember why he is there: not for himself, but for God. He must remember that God chose him because he is the least, not because he is the greatest. He must be a humble servant of the Lord. He must be prepared to allow the love of God to flow through him in his prayer, in his preaching, and in his demeanor toward people. He must love the people entrusted to his care, and he must allow God to love His children through him, His priest.

The material aspect of the priest's preparation for Mass involves preparing the chalice, getting the bread and wine ready, preparing the books, lighting the candles, lighting the coals for the incense (if it is to be used), and properly vesting. Upon arrival at the altar, the priest kisses the altar and incenses it (if the Mass is a High Mass). He needs to be reverent in his prayers in order to bring himself and lead the people deeper and deeper into the mystery of Jesus Christ and His love for us as they prepare to receive the Bridegroom of their souls. United with Jesus in the reception of Holy Communion, they are all given the grace they need to assume the other duties of their lives.

As we have seen, what happens at the parish church also occurs in the domestic church. The man must exercise his priesthood in many ways to serve his family, but the fullest expression of this priesthood within marriage takes place in the sign of the marital covenant. As it is with a priest in the parish, the husband must prepare himself spiritually and materially before he approaches the altar. He must remember that he is not there for himself, but for God and for his wife. He must remember that he was chosen by God and entrusted with the souls of his wife and those in his care. He must therefore strive to be the humble servant, not one who is selfish and arrogant. He must open his heart to love his wife and allow the Lord to love her through him. He must also have his heart open to allow his wife to love him and to allow the Lord to love him through his wife. The love given and received must then be given to all entrusted to his care, especially his children.

As priest of the domestic church, the man must also prepare materially. This preparation is especially toward the altar. Notice at Mass that the altar is passive and receptive. The priest is very active in his duties, but the altar is completely passive at the beginning of Mass. Only at the moment of sacrifice does the altar give forth new life, but it must receive that life before it can give life. So it is in marriage. The husband must prepare the altar, spending much time and energy while the altar is mostly passive and receptive (clearly, not totally passive, as the altar is at Mass). The priest in the marriage, serving the altar, must lead his wife deeper and deeper into the mystery of their love for each other as they prepare to express physically the mystery of their spiritual union. Only at the moment when both sacrifice themselves does the altar give forth new life, but she must receive that life before she can give it. The priest must die to himself and offer himself as the victim on the altar so the altar can receive the sacrifice and offer herself as a victim in return.

Having addressed the priesthood of the husband, we now consider the priesthood of the wife. We have said that the woman is the altar in the domestic church. It should be clear that when we speak of the woman as the altar, we are not in any way equating her with a marble or wooden structure that has no life of its own. There is an ancient saying in the Church: *altare Christus est*—the altar is Christ. This is shown in several ways at Mass but most expressively in the fact that the priest kisses the altar at the beginning and end of Mass. In the Extraordinary Form of the Mass, this reverence is expressed even more strongly: the priest kisses the altar not only at the beginning and end of Mass but every time he comes to the altar and every time he turns away from the altar.

The altar is not only central to the church building: it is also where the central purpose and function of the Church occurs. The altar is dressed in the finest linen, and care is taken to ensure that the altar is always beautiful. Flowers are placed near it to enhance its beauty. Candles are placed on or near the altar; the altar is incensed. People reverence the altar if the Blessed Sacrament is not present. In the Extraordinary Form of the Mass, the readings are done from the altar.

So central is the altar in the life of the Church that it is said: "Everything flows from the altar of God." Indeed, the psalmist says, "Then I will go to the altar of God, to the God of my exceeding joy" (Ps. 43:4). In other words, when we look at everything going on in the Church and in the world, it all flows from the altar of God. From God's perspective, only good—indeed, the greatest good—comes from the altar. However, if the priest or the people desecrate the altar or the fruit of the altar (the Eucharist), then the greatest good God gives us is rejected, and evil is introduced where God was offering His most profound blessing.

Within the domestic church, the wife and mother is clearly central to everything that takes place in the family. Someone once pointed out that a mother knows everything about what each of her children is doing: she knows their friends, their schedules, their likes and dislikes, their struggles, and every last one of their achievements. The father, on the other hand, knows there are some little people populating the house. Life and love, the greatest blessings on both the natural and spiritual planes, come from the woman. As with the altar in the *hieron*, so it is with the altar in the *naos*: if it is desecrated, sin and evil are brought into the place where God intended to give the greatest good. Life and charity can come forth from the wife and mother only if life and charity are allowed to enter and be received. Any intentional obstruction on either the physical or spiritual level desecrates the altar and the fruit of the altar.

God showed the prophet Ezekiel the graces that flowed from the altar. At first, the flow was a runlet; then it grew into a stream and finally into a river. The river itself was teeming with life. Trees grew on either side; their fruit served as food and their leaves served as medicine. These were symbolic of the abundant blessings God would bestow on His people when they kept His Law and made Him the priority of their lives (Ezek. 47:1-12).

Within the domestic church, the greatest blessings flow from the woman. It is within her that life is conceived and nourished, and from her that life flows out into the world. With a mother's heart, she is the vessel of grace for her husband and children. This mirrors God's order of salvation, in which Mary is the mediatrix of all graces. God gives every grace through Mary, and all graces flow through our Blessed Mother. In a marriage, the husband may be the originator of life in the sense that a woman cannot conceive by herself, but once the husband gives this seed of life to his wife, everything else is done in and through her.

It is on the altar that the offerings made to God receive their value. Jesus asked: "For which is greater, the gift or the altar that makes the gift sacred?" (Matt. 23:19). At Mass, the sacrifice of Jesus is offered mystically; on the altar, the death and Resurrection occur. In marriage, if the priest offers his sacrifice in true love, he dies entirely to himself. In response, the altar receives that offering and, offering her sacrifice in true love, dies to herself. Having both died to themselves, their mutual sacrifice is placed upon the altar as the victim (the one whose life is given so another can live); there it is transformed into new life for both spouses. This new life flows from the couple's love for God and for each other and becomes life-giving for others as new life conceived in love or as new life given in service to others. Either way, the fruit of the sacrifice, and therefore the fruit of the altar, is life.

In the Jewish rituals, the priest had to kill the animal that was offered in sacrifice. He then placed the victim on the altar and immolated it as a holocaust. The altar and the victim, in a sense, became one. God received this offering that was made in love and reciprocated by pouring out an abundance of grace for the people. In this ritual, we see that the priest begins with a live victim and sacrifices it, thus placing a dead victim on the altar. The altar receives the dead victim from the priest and, in the immolation, offers the victim to God and receives from Him the divine life of grace. Thus, the pattern of life to death and death to life is revealed.

In marriage, the priest who dies to himself places the dead victim (his self-offering) on the altar; the altar receives the victim, and, immolating the victim by uniting her own death and self-offering to God, she receives grace and new life, which then flow through her and back into the priest. Once again, we see the pattern of death and resurrection.

This mystery of bringing new life from something lifeless can be seen from the beginning: Adam's rib, which had no life of its own, was taken and built into a woman, who was endowed with the fullness of human life (Gen. 2:21–22). The origin of the woman is in death and life; the origin of the marriage is in death and life; the expression of the marriage is in death and life. If the altar was seen as a sepulcher, and the woman is the altar in the temple of the marriage, then the mystery of death and life at work in the woman makes her both a tomb and a womb where the victim is placed and united with the altar and where the transformation from death to life occurs. The altar is all about life, but a death must occur before the life that rises from the altar is revealed. While the expression of the marriage is physical, the death and resurrection that take place on the matrimonial altar is spiritual or, if you will, mystical. Of course, this can be true only if the gift is given and received in love.

In the sacrifices of the Jewish people, God demanded the best. The Jewish people could not offer lambs that were blind, lame, or blemished. Only lambs that were perfect and unblemished were acceptable for sacrifices offered to God. The requirement to offer the best is not because God is selfish or greedy and only wants the best that we have for Himself. Rather, being made in the image and likeness of God, we are made to love, to be loved, and to be transformed into love. The Lord wants us to love Him the way He loves us—that is, with our whole being. Love desires only the best for the other, and so, because we love God, we offer Him the best of what we have and who we are. To offer anything less would be selfish. In the sacrifice of His Son, God gave us the best. He gave us everything and held back nothing. Jesus is the Lamb of God, without blemish, who was sacrificed and sacrificed Himself in love for us.

Similar to the offering made by God, on the day of marriage, the husband and wife did not offer merely the best material possession they had. They offered everything. They offered their whole person to each other. In the sign of their marriage, this offering is renewed. The conjugal act should be a physical *re-pronunciation* of the marriage vows. In this offering, each person offers his or her entire self to the other and, together, they offer the gift of their entire selves to God. The vow in marriage is to love the other, and so the physical expression of that vow must be an act of love. It is to seek only the best for the other and not to be self-seeking.

Our society has made conjugal relations into a pastime in which all that matters is how much satisfaction and pleasure you can obtain for yourself from the other person. This is a perversion of God's intention for the marital act. In fact, beyond being a perversion, it is an inversion of God's intention. Rather than being two people giving and receiving each other in an act of true charity, it is two people selfishly using each other for their own pleasure and satisfaction. Because of what has become the societal norm, it may seem foreign to think of this act of union as a sacrifice. But recall the meaning of the word *sacrifice*: "to make holy." If the gift is not a sacrifice, it is not holy. In other words, if either the priest, the altar, or both are not exercising their proper function, the offering, the victim, is not acceptable and is not holy.

<hr />

Questions for Reflection

1. As a husband, how do you fulfill your office as priest? As a wife, how do you fulfill your office as altar?
2. As a husband, how can you honor your wife as a priest honors the altar? As a wife, how can you honor your husband as you would a priest?
3. What is the most powerful lesson you have learned from your spouse in his or her office as prophet (teacher)?
4. When you exercise the office of king (servant), are you joyful? Are you glad to be helping your family? If not, how can you be a grateful servant like our Lord?

7

The Banquet of the Lamb

It's no coincidence that our Lord began His public ministry at a wedding banquet. When we look at the end of His life, He completed His public ministry at a marriage feast—that is, in the consummation of His marriage to His Bride, the Church. We know that in Holy Matrimony the marriage ends with the death of one of the spouses. However, with our Lord and the Church, the marriage began with the death of the Bridegroom, resulting in the *creation* of His Bride. Heaven is revealed to us as a marriage banquet (Rev. 19:7-9; 21:9), and since the Church transcends time and space, she has already entered into Heaven in the persons of the saints. The marriage that began on Calvary is lived forever in eternity.

Going back to the beginning of our Lord's public ministry, not only is Cana associated with a wedding, but, in the changing of water into wine, Cana is also associated with the Eucharist. The pinnacle of our Lord's ministry, which took place on the Cross, is associated with a wedding, but in the pouring out of His Blood, it is also associated with the Eucharist. Even more clearly, on the night prior to His Crucifixion, Jesus offered sacramentally and mystically the exact same sacrifice that He offered physically on the Cross the next day. In many aspects, the Eucharist and the marriage of our Lord are the same; it is not possible to have a deeper understanding of one without reference to the other.

Before looking at the correlation between the Holy Eucharist and Holy Matrimony, we need to understand that all the sacraments are related to the Eucharist. That's because the Eucharist, being the very Flesh and Blood of Jesus Christ, is the source and summit of all the sacraments and of the Christian life. At the same time, each of the sacraments is related to and builds upon Baptism because none of the other sacraments can be received until a person is baptized. Some relationships between the various sacraments are easy to see. For example, Confirmation completes Baptism, and the relationship between Holy Orders and the Eucharist is quite obvious.

The relationship between Baptism, the Eucharist, and Holy Matrimony is the most intriguing because only these three sacraments are covenants. In each of these covenants, there is an incorporation into a person and a participation in the life of the other person. In Baptism and Holy Communion, that participation is on a supernatural level, whereas in Holy Matrimony, it is on the natural level. We have spoken about the connections between Baptism and the Eucharist and also the correlations between Baptism and Matrimony. We have mentioned some of the points of conjunction between Matrimony and the Eucharist, but we need to look at the relationship between these two sacraments more closely.

It was mentioned earlier that a deeper understanding of either the Holy Eucharist or Holy Matrimony is not possible without reference to the other. So much has been written about each of these sacraments over the centuries. What St. John said at the end of his Gospel regarding the words and works of Jesus, "the world itself could not contain the books that would be written" (John 21:25), can be said about both of these sacraments, but especially about the Eucharist, because the Eucharist is Jesus Himself. For every Catholic person, a love for and an understanding of (to the degree of our ability) the Eucharist is necessary. For the married couple, however, their relationship to the Eucharist not only helps them to know Jesus and to know themselves as persons made in His image and likeness, but it informs their marital relationship. This is true regarding people in any state in life, but of all the sacraments, the Eucharist and Matrimony are the two most closely related, symbolically. The symbolism is identical in so many ways, albeit on two levels. This cannot be said of any other sacrament or state in life.

For instance, each sacrament, to be valid, requires the proper matter, form, and intention. The matter for the Eucharist requires two distinct elements: bread and wine. The matter for Holy Matrimony also requires two distinct elements: a male and a female. If a Mass were attempted using two hosts and no wine, or using two chalices of wine and no host, the Mass would be invalid. Likewise, the primary end of the Mass is the sacrifice of Jesus and His presence in the Holy Eucharist. Two of the same elements can neither fully express the sacrifice nor produce supernatural life in the Eucharist. If a marriage were attempted between two men or two women, the marriage would be invalid. We saw earlier that the first end of marriage is children, and obviously two persons of the same sex cannot bring forth new life.

In chapter 6, we saw that the Church and the Eucharist are mutually dependent. The Church has life and existence through Christ and through the offering of His sacrifice. Our Lord has life and existence in the Eucharist through the Church and through the offering of her sacrifice, which is also His sacrifice. Neither can exist without the other. The same is true in marriage. Just as Jesus existed before the Church was founded, so the two persons who marry exist before their marriage. However, their existence as husband and wife comes through and is dependent on the other person. As a married couple, neither can exist without the other.

The form, or the words that are spoken, are also necessary for the validity of the sacrament. However, when we look at both the Holy Eucharist and Holy Matrimony, the words necessary for validity also have another purpose: they express love. Normally, we would say love is expressed through actions. We can certainly see our Lord's love for us in His actions, especially on the Cross. But we believe in the Holy Eucharist not because of anything we can see but because Jesus said it. Of course, we can look at some of the Eucharistic miracles that have occurred over the centuries, but these are usually given because people do not believe. We have faith in the Eucharist not because of the miracles but because Jesus said the bread and wine are His Body and Blood. The same is true regarding marriage. One can consider all the things a couple does for each other that demonstrate their love, but the union of marriage is real not because of the service each spouse provides to the other but because of the words spoken in the vows that express the intention of the heart.

Receiving love is much more difficult than giving love because we can control what we give but we cannot control what the other person gives. This being the case, it can be very difficult for us to believe that someone actually loves us as much as that person's words declare. Jesus' words spoken at the Consecration are absolute: "This is my Body"; "This is the chalice of my Blood." The words spoken in the marriage vows are also absolute: "I will love you and honor you all the days of my life." Notice there is no qualifier. The words do not proclaim that "I love you a lot," or "I love you so much." The vow to love is absolute, whereas any qualification reduces the love that is vowed and lived. A married person should bring this to prayer and allow this truth to sink deeply into his or her heart.

This brings us to consider the disposition of our Lord in the Holy Eucharist. He is present for one reason only: because He loves us. His disposition at the Consecration is pure charity, and His disposition in giving Himself in Holy Communion is pure charity. His disposition in the tabernacle or in the monstrance for adoration is pure charity. His disposition never changes. Regardless of the moment or the action, Jesus is always giving Himself completely. Charity, as we have seen, requires both giving and receiving. Therefore, our Lord's disposition in receiving the gift we give Him is also pure charity. He will not reject anything of what we give Him.

Because the Church transcends our world of time, we can say that time enters into eternity in the Mystical Person of the Church. In the same manner, we can say that in the Eucharist, eternity enters into time in the Person of Jesus. Jesus is the Bridegroom of our souls, so in the Eucharist, He is not only present but He gives Himself to us as the Bridegroom. In the previous chapter, when we spoke of the union of Jesus and the Church, we said that the disposition of the Bride and the Bridegroom are identical: pure charity. As members of the Church and, therefore, members of the Bride, we need to be sure that when we receive into ourselves the Bridegroom of our souls, we have the same disposition in receiving Him as He has in giving Himself to us. Also, for those who are called to the vocation of marriage, the disposition of bride and groom should mirror the disposition Jesus has as He gives Himself to us in the Eucharist and as He receives our gift of self to Him. Every married person must learn from the love of Jesus in the Eucharist and apply this love to his or her own marriage. We must understand that this love applies not only to the intimacy of marital relations, because, as we saw in chapter 5, the intimate aspect of marriage is a microcosm of the whole marriage. While this disposition must be present in sexual intimacy, it must be the norm for every aspect of the marriage before it can be expressed as the norm in the most intimate aspect of the marriage.

This disposition of our Lord in the Holy Eucharist is, perhaps, what married people need to meditate on the most, because it is the same disposition they have vowed to each other. Sometimes our disposition changes with the situation or with our emotions. Jesus does not change His disposition even if someone hates Him or disbelieves Him. Love, recall, is a virtue. This means it does not change, even when our emotions change. Our Lord's love cannot grow because it is absolutely perfect; however, the love of a couple in marriage can and must grow. When love grows, it does not change—it develops and is perfected. Love, by its nature, either increases or decreases, but it never remains the same. So, if our love is not growing, it is diminishing. Sometimes it may feel as if one's love is going in the wrong direction because of the struggles and difficulties that arise in marriage. But love grows the most when it seems the most difficult to love. It may not feel as if love is growing, but love is not based on feelings. If one continues to try to treat the other with kindness and respect, serves the other, and seeks only what is best for the other when it is difficult, this is when the love is proven and when it excels.

Needless to say, this is very difficult. But on the day of marriage, a couple does not vow to have happy feelings toward each other, to love each other only when things are going well. Hopefully they don't expect a fairy-tale ending of living happily ever after, because that doesn't exist. True happiness comes only when their union has been purified in the crucible of suffering and proven in adversity.

For this to happen, it is necessary for the couple to pray for each other. It's easy to forget to pray for each other throughout the day, but prayer is the greatest work of love. So praying for each other—and praying to love each other more—not only helps the other person by obtaining grace for them; it also helps the one praying by keeping the disposition of an open heart toward the other.

Of course, it can be very difficult to pray for someone when we are angry with that person or when there is some kind of division in the relationship. But regardless of the situation, there can be no actual division in a marriage. After all, the two are really one! Neither can there be a waning in either the prayer for the other or in the love one has for the other.

What we're talking about here, after all, is sacrifice. And before the Holy Eucharist can be a sacrament, it too must be a sacrifice. Jesus had to sacrifice Himself in order to give Himself to us in the Blessed Sacrament. This sacrifice of Jesus is a complete and total self-giving. He gave Himself completely and absolutely on the Cross; in the Eucharist, He continues to give Himself completely, holding nothing back. This sacrifice and this total self-giving make this a gift of true and perfect love.

In order for a couple to enter into the sacrament of Holy Matrimony, they each offer themselves as a complete and total sacrifice to each other. As with the sacrifice of our Lord, this must be a total self-giving, holding nothing back. If only a small or partial sacrifice is made, only a portion of the person would be given. If this were the situation, the vows would be false, and the sacrament would be invalid. It needs to be made clear that each person can give himself or herself only to the degree of his or her capacity. In other words, each person gives himself or herself completely to the other on their wedding day, but as the love grows in the marriage, each day there should be more to give. Since nothing was held back in the beginning, the couple gave everything they were at that moment, which included everything they would be in the future.

Our Lord's giving was absolutely perfect from the beginning, but ours can be only relatively perfect — that is, giving as perfectly as we are able. St. Bernard of Clairvaux said, "Nothing is lacking where everything is given."[4] If two people give themselves completely on the day of their marriage, they are not holding anything back selfishly. If, each day, they have a greater capacity to love, this greater love was not withheld previously; it was given as part of the potential of who the person would become. Therefore, at each moment, the two persons love each other with a greater capacity, always giving themselves completely and holding nothing back. As it is with our Lord's sacrifice, so it is with the sacrifice in marriage: it is a total gift of true love with no selfishness.

All of this is part of the intention, the third aspect required to make the marriage valid. The intention of the couple to a loving, life-giving sacrifice is the same intention our Lord has in the Holy Eucharist. This intention becomes critical for the couple to implement in the intimacy of their relationship because, as we have seen, the sexual union of the couple is a physical re-pronunciation of the vows. The couple's intention had to be correct on their wedding day for the marriage to be valid. This same intention must be present when the husband and wife approach each other to express their spiritual union physically and to re-pronounce in a physical way their vow of love for each other.

Sterilization or the use of contraceptives is a clear statement regarding the intent of the couple in the marital act. It would be similar to a priest who approaches the altar for Mass properly vested and says the right words but has no intention to consecrate

[4] Sermon 83.

the Eucharist. The bread and wine remain just bread and wine. There is no Mass, and no true expression of the priesthood. For the married couple, anything sinful in the sexual part of their relationship renders the act incomplete. There is no true expression of their sacrament. To do anything sinful with or to one's spouse robs the union of its sacrifice. This selfishness becomes the thief of the sacrifice and causes the holocaust to be invalid. This is tantamount to Satan's declaration, "I will not serve." It is the opposite of Moses' plea when he placed before the people life and death, the blessing and the curse, and exhorted them to choose life (Deut. 30:19). Recall that, for the couple, this life is given to each other whether or not a baby is conceived.

For the married couple, choosing life becomes a major test of their love and fidelity toward each other and toward God. Our society tells people that contraception makes sense. To this I would say two things. First, loving each other makes sense; using each other does not make sense. Second, when the angels fell it was, in part, because God's plan did not make sense to them and they would not accept what they could not understand. If we are going to be tested by God, it will be about what is right and true, but it will not be easy. For married couples, God's plan is expressed in the covenant: permanence, fidelity, and openness to life.

When we consider our salvation, we recognize that Jesus was obedient even unto death (Phil. 2:8). Even with this knowledge, it can be a challenge for us to understand how this can be God's plan for our salvation. Peter did not understand this at first, either. In fact, he rebuked Jesus when our Lord told His apostles He would have to suffer and die (Matt. 16:22; Mark 8:32). From Peter's very limited perspective, even though he had just declared Jesus to be the Messiah and he knew from his knowledge of Scripture that the Messiah had to suffer and die, the wisdom of God expressed in Jesus' words made no sense to him at that time. After receiving the Holy Spirit on the day of Pentecost, we see Peter presenting this same mystery from a completely different perspective. After witnessing Jesus' Resurrection and receiving the promised gift of the Holy Spirit, he had come to understand Jesus' words and was then able to tell the people that Jesus was crucified by the set plan and foreknowledge of God (Acts 2:23). What made no sense to Peter at an earlier date suddenly made perfect sense when seen from God's perspective.

Holy Matrimony is a divine mystery. We can grasp certain aspects of marriage with relative ease. Other aspects seem difficult to understand. However, when we look at things from God's perspective rather than from our own very limited perspectives, things begin to become clearer. Sometimes, we are asked simply to accept with faith that the understanding will come at a later date. At other times, we are given clarity to embrace the situation and live it out fully with the greatest charity. Regardless, we know God's ways are perfect, even if they are beyond our ability to comprehend fully. For this reason, like Jesus, we want to exercise obedience to God's plan for our lives and our vocations and trust that He will work all things for good (see Rom. 8:28).

Applying this same line of thought to the Eucharist, many people cannot accept that Jesus gives Himself to us in the form of a piece of bread. If we consider this only from a perspective of what makes logical sense and what we can perceive with our senses, we would reject the truth of the Eucharist outright. However, when we look at this from the perspective of love, then it makes perfect sense. Our Lord is the Bridegroom of our souls, so He wants to have a way to express His union with us. We have to accept that He spoke the truth and that He loves us this much. Married couples often express the wish that they could somehow get inside the other person because they love each other that much. Jesus is God;

He loves us infinitely more than we can love one another, so He has provided a way to give Himself so perfectly that He can enter into us: into our hearts and souls. When we receive Jesus in Holy Communion, we also need to accept and receive His love and His desire to be united with us.

Remember, too, that Satan and his angels fell because God's plan for salvation didn't "make sense" to them. Oftentimes in our lives, we're called to set aside our own misgivings and to trust in God, who can neither mislead nor be misled. That's the very definition of faith: letting Christ lead us by the hand when we can't see.

You must have faith in your spouse too. On the day of your marriage, you spoke vows to each other. Both of you need to accept that the other person spoke the truth and that your spouse loves you. At the same time, each of you must receive the love of the other that is expressed in countless ways throughout the day but finds its highest expression in your physical intimacy. Each of you must accept and receive the life the other person is offering as a sacrifice of love. Sometimes, the way one's spouse loves or needs to be loved is difficult for us to understand and, consequently, is ignored or rejected. Only when considered from the perspective of truly loving the other by seeking what is best for that person will we understand and adjust to the way the other person loves or needs to be loved.

We know that our Lord is present in the fullness of His Person in the Holy Eucharist. When we want to tell someone that we give our entire person to him or her, we often say, "I give you my heart." There are several documented miracles in which the Host has physically turned into a piece of flesh.[5] The Church has allowed

---

[5] See Dr. Franco Serafini, *A Cardiologist Examines Jesus: The Stunning Science behind Eucharistic Miracles* (Manchester, NH: Sophia Institute Press, 2021).

scientific investigations of these phenomena. Many things can be ascertained that correspond to our belief in the Real Presence, but the aspect of these occurrences that I find most fascinating is that the flesh is cardiac tissue. The only part of the human body made of cardiac tissue, of course, is the heart. We know the Eucharist is the Body, Blood, Soul, and Divinity of Jesus, but when He causes the accidents of the bread to change into His flesh, He gives us His Heart to reveal His love for us and to show that He gives Himself entirely to us.

Another beautiful correlation between Matrimony and the Eucharist is that, in marriage, the couple do not give gifts to each other on their wedding day because they *are* the gift they give to each other. In His marriage to the Church in general, and to our souls in particular, Jesus gives Himself to us as a gift, and each of us gives our self to Him as a gift. Once again, this should cause the married person to meditate on the disposition of Jesus as He gives Himself to us in Holy Communion and as He receives us as a gift in Holy Communion. Recall His words from the Gospel of John: "Father, they are your gift to me" (see 17:24).

Perhaps the most wonderful correlation between Holy Matrimony and the Holy Eucharist is that both mysteries foreshadow and prefigure Heaven. On one hand, Heaven will be the Mass in which the Lamb of God will be given to the saints always and forever. On the other hand, Heaven will be a wedding where the Lamb of God will be given to the saints always and forever. Of course, the saints will not only receive the Lamb and His love; they will also give themselves in love to the Lamb.

Heaven is a marriage banquet, and Jesus is the Bridegroom, so it makes sense that when Heaven comes to Earth and eternity enters into time, Heaven is recognized in the context of a wedding. This is exactly what happens every time Jesus makes Himself present to us at Mass: it is the marriage supper of the Lamb. This is what we hear in the Ordinary Form of the Mass immediately prior to receiving Holy Communion, when the priest holds up the Host and pronounces the words of St. John the Baptist, "Behold the Lamb of God," and then proclaims: "Blessed are those who are called to the supper of the Lamb." This is a passage from the book of Revelation, and it refers to the marriage banquet or supper of Jesus (Rev. 19:9). If Heaven will be both Mass and marriage, then the prefiguration of this is found both in the Mass and in Matrimony. Therefore, the fullness of Heaven is prefigured in a Nuptial Mass.

The life of Heaven is also foreshadowed in the reception of Holy Communion by the faithful. Not only is receiving Holy Communion a prefiguration of our union with Jesus for eternity: it also foreshadows the union of all the faithful in Heaven. In the heavenly marriage banquet, the Bride is the communion of all the saints, who are united together by the bonds of grace and charity. So each soul is united with our Lord, but each person in Heaven is also united with one another. In Heaven, there will be only charity. Every person will be loving God and loving every other person perfectly, and each person will be loved by God and loved by every other person perfectly. Needless to say, in marriage, this union is foreshadowed in the union of the two persons. Although marriage ends at the moment one of the spouses dies, this is not because marriage is somehow flawed but because marriage prefigures and prepares the married persons for Heaven.

Marriage on Earth is the union of husband and wife, bridegroom and bride; marriage in Heaven is the union of the Bridegroom and the Bride. But in Heaven, the Bride comprises the countless persons united as one in the Communion of Saints. This union is what we see foreshadowed in Holy Communion. Each person who receives Communion in the state of grace is united with Jesus. However, that person is also united with every other person who receives Holy Communion throughout the world. This is true because each of these persons is united to Jesus, so each person united to Jesus is also united with one another. This mystical union of the faithful that we experience now through grace and charity, especially in the reception of the Eucharist, prefigures the union we will enjoy eternally in Heaven. This reality also calls each of us to a deeper conversion, not only so we can be more perfectly united with our Lord but also because we are called to love each person who loves our Lord and is loved by our Lord. Just as spouses are to grow in love for each other each day, so our love for God and our neighbor must grow each day. This is especially true regarding people we may not like. If we are united with them now in the Eucharist, and we hope to be united with them for eternity in the marriage of Heaven, then we need to develop charity toward them now so we can love them in the Lord for all eternity.

Of course, to have this love for everyone is very difficult. So, in His providence, God gives a husband and wife to each other to teach them how to love as He loves. When a husband and wife go to Mass and receive our Lord in Holy Communion, one thing they should ponder is this: "If my spouse is so lovable that Jesus loves him [or her] *that* much, I should be loving him [or her] in the same manner." With each reception of Holy Communion, husband and wife should grow closer to Jesus and to each other because both are united with Jesus, and both should be loving Jesus more and receiving more of His love. Since it is the Lord who united the couple in marriage and remains in that union, the union and the love of the couple should also grow because of their deeper union with the Lord.

As we have seen, love cannot remain in just the two; love must overflow the boundaries of the couple and extend to others. We must also remember that we cannot initiate love; we can only respond to it. God loves us first, and then, receiving His love, we can love Him in return and love others with the same love God has given to us. St. John says: "In this is love, not that we loved God but that he loved us" (1 John 4:10). This being the order of love, the more we love God, the more we can love others. The order is simple: God, spouse, children, others. If you want to love your spouse more, love God more first. If you want to love your children more, love your spouse more. The greater love you have for our Lord in the Blessed Sacrament (who loves you perfectly), the greater will be your ability to love your spouse. The greater your capacity to love your spouse, the greater capacity you have to love your children. The greater your capacity to love your children, the greater capacity you have to love your neighbor.

We've seen that Jesus, who is eternal, entered into time. We've also seen that the Church, which is temporal, enters into eternity. The point of connection between time and eternity can be understood in two ways. First, in the Incarnation of our Lord, the Creator becomes a creature and the eternal becomes temporal. This establishes the means for humanity to participate in the divinity and for those bound by death to live as children of God in the glory of eternal life. The second point of connection, and the one that allows for this transformation, is the Cross. The Cross unites Heaven and Earth, time and eternity. It is wonderful that God became man and that Heaven entered into the earthly realm, but, by itself, this connection does not redeem us or open the way for man to become one with God and for the earthly to enter the heavenly realm. The Cross, like a bridge, stretches over the chasm separating Heaven and Earth and reconciles what appears to be irreconcilable and unites what appears to be disunited.

The Cross has two beams: a vertical beam that points upward, representing Heaven, and a horizontal beam representing the earth. On these two beams is nailed the One who has two natures, divine and human. The One who united divinity and humanity in Himself, the One who united eternity and time in Himself, the One who united Heaven and Earth in Himself, is united to the Cross, suspended between Heaven and Earth.

Not only is the Cross like the key that opens the doorway to Heaven for us, but it is also the means by which God has chosen to give us His life. Jesus gave His life on the Cross, so it makes sense that His life will flow into us from the Cross. This is certainly what we have seen with the creation of the Church, the Bride of the Lamb, who was poured forth from the opened side of our Savior as He hung upon the Cross in death. This life of Christ continues to flow into and through the Church to all who are her children. When we go back to the Garden of Eden and recall the sin of Adam and Eve and its punishment, we saw that life would come into the world through women in pain, and life would be sustained by men in pain. In other words, the man's task is to provide the food that will sustain the life of his wife and children. Jesus, the new Adam, has done exactly that. In most marriages, the mother prepares the meals for the family, but traditionally, the man has had to work to obtain the food. In God's family, the Church prepares the food (the Holy Eucharist) for her children, but it is her Bridegroom who has done the work to provide the food that will sustain the life of the souls of the children.

In the garden, Adam and Eve did not eat of the fruit of the Tree of Life; but, in a garden two thousand years ago, the Cross became the Tree of Life. The Cross is life-giving not only for the Church, but through the Church, the Bride of the Lamb, the Cross is life-giving for all her children. The fruit of the Tree of Life is the Eucharist. The Cross was planted physically in the earth so our Redeemer could be mystically crucified on it. Scripture tells us the Cross is now in Heaven (Rev. 2:7; 22:2, 14). Because Heaven is on Earth in the Person of Jesus Christ, and Earth is in Heaven in both Jesus and in the saints, it is possible for the fruit of the Tree of Life to be present mystically on Earth. In the Holy Eucharist, the fruit of the Tree of Life is mystically (that is, sacramentally) present to us so we can eat of it and never die (see John 6:50). As we saw earlier, the Eucharist is the sacramental presence of the Lord. Christ is present because His sacrifice, offered physically on the Cross, continues to be offered mystically at Mass.

At Mass, each person is united with our Lord in His suffering and in His glory. We are united with Him in His suffering when the priest prays that "my sacrifice and yours may be acceptable to God, the Almighty Father." Jesus does not suffer in the Holy Eucharist, but sacrifice and suffering cannot be separated. Therefore, with the sacrifice being offered mystically, the suffering is offered mystically as well, through the Mystical Body of Christ. This means that each person can bring his or her struggles and sufferings to Mass and place them on the paten with the bread and pour them in the chalice with the wine. Then, at the Consecration, each person's suffering is united to the sacrifice of Christ and becomes His suffering.

Each person who worthily receives Holy Communion is united with our Lord in His glory, because, as we saw earlier, Jesus is present in the Holy Eucharist as He is right now, that is, in His glory at the right hand of the Father in Heaven. In the book of Revelation, Jesus says He will give the victor, or the one who conquers, the fruit of the Tree of Life (Rev. 2:7). Jesus is the Victor over sin and death. When we are united with Jesus, we participate in that victory over sin and death. And so, provided we remain united with

Him to the end—that is, provided we die in the state of grace—we will enter into the victory celebration of Heaven, where we will be victorious through, with, and in Christ. What is this victory celebration? It is the marriage banquet of the Lamb!

If the victory celebration is in Heaven, and marriage foreshadows Heaven, then the victory celebration is already present in marriages that reflect and participate in the life of Heaven. Each spouse has offered himself or herself as a sacrifice to God and to each other, so this reflects our Lord's offering of Himself as a sacrifice. Each spouse should be working to love his or her spouse more, which requires a dying to self. The suffering required for this self-immolation and the failures we have in denying ourselves to love the other are part of the suffering we can offer at Mass. The more generous we are in offering ourselves, the more we will be able to receive from the generosity of our Lord, who receives our gift and reciprocates by giving us the gift of Himself. Then, with a heart filled more completely with the love of God, each spouse can respond to God with the love He has put into his or her heart.

God has given married couples the profound gift of being able to fulfill the purpose of their creation through, with, and in each other. We have merely scratched the surface of this spiritual mystery, a mystery that is deep and glorious, ever ancient and ever new. As beautiful as this is, we have to see marriage in its proper and eternal context. Marriage, as we know, is not an end in itself. It is the way of becoming saints and raising new saints for God. It is a gift given from the beginning and, in the marriage of the Lamb, it is a gift that will endure for all eternity. Holy Matrimony prefigures and foreshadows Heaven, but, at the same time, it already participates and makes present the life of Heaven on Earth.

In the beginning, everything God created reflected His perfection. Everything was created out of love for us, and we were created to love God and one another. Prior to the Fall, life in the Garden of Eden was not merely a reflection of the life of Heaven but was a *participation* in the life of Heaven. Adam and Eve possessed grace and walked with God. Everything was in perfect order and harmony and centered on the Tree of Life in the middle of the Garden. Life in the garden was pure charity.

By living their lives on Earth in union with God, Adam and Eve were not only fulfilling the purpose of their being. They were also fulfilling each other by loving each other as perfectly as they could at every moment with the love they received from God. In the garden, God was with His creatures, eternity had entered into time, and the life of Heaven was present on Earth. But by choosing selfishness over love, the first couple rejected God and His love for them. They brought disorder into creation. They were ejected from the garden because they had ejected God and His grace from the garden of their souls.

Heaven was no longer on Earth. All that remained was a reflection found in the human persons, who were created in the image and likeness of God.

God promised Adam and Eve a Redeemer, and He began preparing humanity for their redemption. In the proper time, He chose a people for Himself and entered into covenants with them. With the revelations God gave to Moses, the life of Heaven could be reflected and imitated on Earth. Moses was shown the worship of Heaven and told to make a Temple in the pattern of what he had seen (Exod. 25-31). We see this pattern in the Jewish offering of a lamb for the forgiveness of their sins. We also see the life of Heaven reflected in the Jewish understanding of marriage. As we have seen, Jewish marriages are based on the covenant God made with Moses. After Moses was graced with the vision of Heaven, the Hebrew understanding of marriage changed to reflect and imitate what Moses saw in this vision. A Jewish marriage, recall, was a week-long celebration, no doubt to reflect the seven days of creation. Marriage was central to the original creation, and it would be central to the new creation, so it makes sense that God wanted the Jewish people to imitate and reflect the original creation in their marriages in order to prepare them for the new creation.

When Jesus came in the fullness of time to fulfill the promises of God and to unite Heaven and Earth, He reestablished true worship and participation in the life of Heaven on Earth through grace and the sacraments. Moses made a pattern of what he saw, but the Lamb he saw in Heaven was Jesus. The marriage banquet he saw was the marriage of the Lamb and His Bride. The Holy Eucharist not only foreshadows and prefigures Heaven: it already participates in the life of Heaven on Earth. Holy Matrimony foreshadows and prefigures the marriage banquet of Heaven, but it is already a participation in the life of Heaven. Along with the covenants and mutual incorporations we have seen, we can say that we are given grace, the life of God, in Baptism; we have union with God in the Holy Eucharist; and we have union with one another in Holy Matrimony.

The order and perfection of the Garden of Eden have not been fully restored because the effects of sin remain. Nevertheless, with the forgiveness of our sins, we can be reconciled with God. Once again, God can dwell with His human creatures. Grace and charity have been restored, and we can live the way we were created to live. Marriage was never taken away from humanity. Rather, marriage has not only been restored to its original dignity but has been elevated beyond what it was in the beginning in the garden.

As it was in the Garden of Eden, married couples are to love God and love each other. They are to reflect the love of the Most

Holy Trinity, and, even more, they are to allow the Persons of the Trinity to love in and through them because the Trinity dwells within them. This was the grace Adam and Eve possessed and were to pass on to their children.

The full dignity of married life is found only in the revelation of the marriage banquet of the Lamb. The sacrificial love of Jesus in the Eucharist and His union with His Bride that was established through His sacrifice provide the full context for understanding the dignity of Holy Matrimony. Husband and wife sacrifice themselves out of love for God and each other; through this sacrificial love, God unites the couple to share in His love and in His creative work. Heaven entered into Earth when God worked the miracle of uniting the two persons to be one, and He remains in that union as long as grace and charity are present. The fulfillment of this love will bring the couple to the fullness of life and love in Heaven, where everything they reflected and participated in during their married life on Earth will find its perfection.

As members of the Bride, they will fulfill in Heaven what they began on Earth. In Heaven, each person will give himself or herself in perfect love to Jesus and to every other person who is a member of the Bride, and each person will receive perfect love from Jesus and from every other person in Heaven. Earth enters into Heaven in the persons of these blessed souls, who immerse themselves in the fullness of what their marriages on Earth prefigured and foreshadowed. Called by the Bridegroom of their souls, everything will be perfectly ordered, and everything will be pure charity as they enter into eternal joy and enjoy the eternal marriage banquet of the Lamb that was prepared for them from the beginning, the Eucharist of eternal Love. Truly blessed are those called to the marriage banquet of the Lamb!

Questions for Reflection

1. What are some ways you and your spouse or your family could grow in devotion to the Holy Eucharist?'

2. "In most marriages, the mother prepares the meals for the family, but traditionally, the man has had to work to obtain the food." How does your work complement that of your spouse? What are some ways in which you *don't* cooperate well, and how may you overcome that friction?

3. Does your marriage feel like a "loving, life-giving sacrifice"?

4. Have the trials and joys of marriage taught you anything about *agape* love? Have you learned to love your neighbor better by learning to love your husband or wife?

5. What is the most interesting or useful lesson you learned from this book? How are you going to apply it to your marriage—right now?

Acknowledgments

My gratitude is extended to everyone who had a part in getting this book to press. I will list the people who helped me directly in chronological order. Before I began writing, I had two questions, one about covenants and one regarding the Hebrew language. I wrote to Dr. Scott Hahn, whom I have never had the honor to meet or even speak with, and he kindly responded and answered my questions. Don Fier provided me with the work he had done, which was incorporated into the third chapter. When the writing was done, a dear friend, who wishes to remain anonymous, did the tremendous work of the first and second edits on the manuscript. After that, my extraordinary secretary, Mary Fier, and her husband, Don, read the manuscript and provided more edits. I then sent it to another dear friend, Sue Zappa, who did the final editing work. Once the editing was done, I sent the manuscript to Fr. Cassian de Rocco, who holds a doctorate in Marriage and Family. He painstakingly went through the first three chapters, which are the foundational chapters, and helped me make the proper distinctions. When he had a question about a theological point, he sought the help of Dr. Joseph Arias, a theology professor at Christendom College. The help these men provided was invaluable. I and my readers am most grateful to all these individuals for their kindness, their feedback, and their help. The final version is far more readable than the original.

When everything was finally in order, Ann Virnig put me in touch with the people at Sophia Institute Press to get the production started. Charlie McKinney and his staff at the press have been extremely patient and wonderful to work with. Dan and Stephanie Burke helped with opening the doors at Sophia Institute Press and very generously agreed to write the foreword for this book.

About the Author

Fr. Robert Altier is a priest of the Archdiocese of St. Paul and Minneapolis in Minnesota. He was ordained in 1989 and is currently the parochial vicar at the Church of the Holy Trinity in South St. Paul.

Fr. Altier taught the comprehensive sixty-part catechetical series *Beauty, Truth, Goodness: The Fundamentals of Catholicism*, which has been aired on eight Catholic television networks throughout North America, Mexico, and Central America. He has been a frequent contributor on Relevant Radio. He wrote an examination of conscience that has been very popular for a number of years and is available in both English and Spanish.

Fr. Altier is president of Help the Helpless, an organization that raises funds to support handicapped orphans in India and the poorest of the poor in Ecuador (helpthehelpless.org); he is chairman of the board of the Holy Family Catholic Adoption Agency, a truly Catholic adoption agency working to end abortion through adoption (holyfamilyadoption.org); he is the spiritual director of

Catholic Parents Online, which seeks to ensure, promote, and defend authentic Catholic teaching in schools and the wider community (catholicparents.org). Fr. Altier has been a member of the Secular Order of Discalced Carmelites since 1983.

Sophia Institute

Sophia Institute is a nonprofit institution that seeks to nurture the spiritual, moral, and cultural life of souls and to spread the gospel of Christ in conformity with the authentic teachings of the Roman Catholic Church.

Sophia Institute Press fulfills this mission by offering translations, reprints, and new publications that afford readers a rich source of the enduring wisdom of mankind.

Sophia Institute also operates the popular online resource CatholicExchange.com. *Catholic Exchange* provides world news from a Catholic perspective as well as daily devotionals and articles that will help readers to grow in holiness and live a life consistent with the teachings of the Church.

In 2013, Sophia Institute launched Sophia Institute for Teachers to renew and rebuild Catholic culture through service to Catholic education. With the goal of nurturing the spiritual, moral, and cultural life of souls, and an abiding respect for the role and work of teachers, we strive to provide materials and programs that are at once enlightening to the mind and ennobling to the heart; faithful and complete, as well as useful and practical.

Sophia Institute gratefully recognizes the Solidarity Association for preserving and encouraging the growth of our apostolate over the course of many years. Without their generous and timely support, this book would not be in your hands.

www.SophiaInstitute.com
www.CatholicExchange.com
www.SophiaInstituteforTeachers.org

Sophia Institute Press is a registered trademark of Sophia Institute.
Sophia Institute is a tax-exempt institution as defined by the
Internal Revenue Code, Section 501(c)(3). Tax ID 22-2548708.